The interior decorator, being the laws of harmonious coloring adapted to interior decorations with observations on the practice of house painting - Primary Source Edition

Hay, D. R

DIAGRAM
OF THE
PRIMARY, SECONDARY & TERTIARY COLOURS

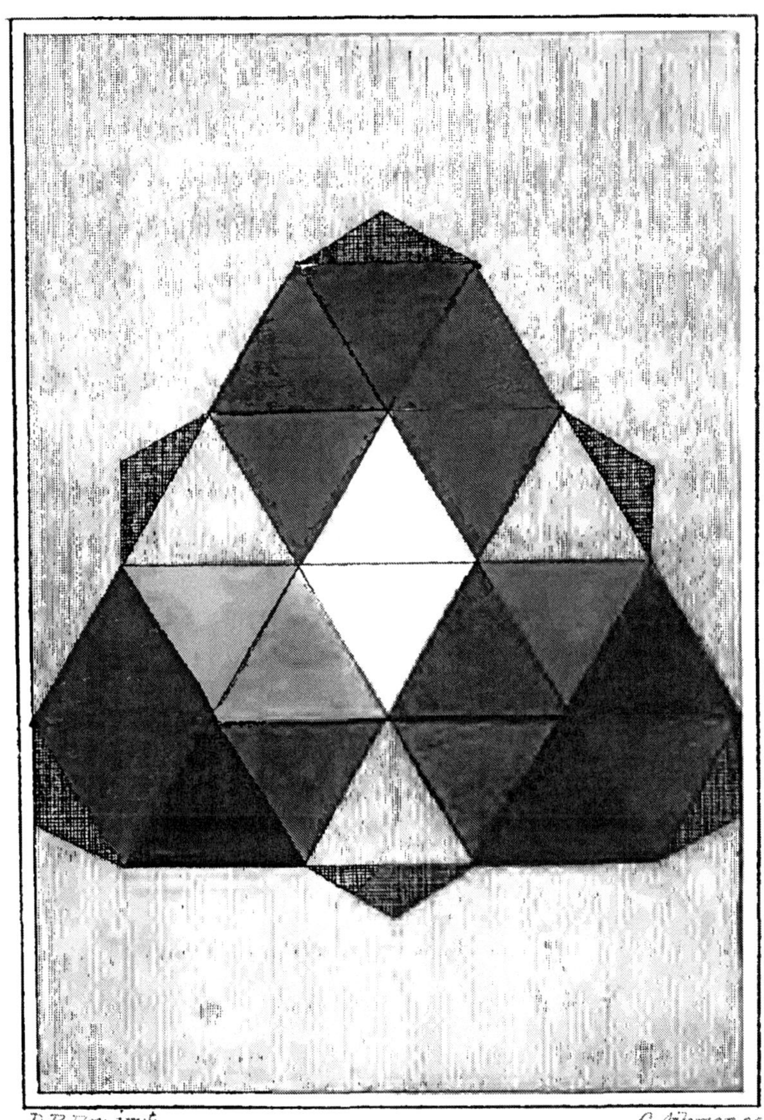

D. R. Hay invt — *G. Aikman sc*

THE

INTERIOR DECORATOR,

BEING THE

LAWS OF HARMONIOUS COLORING

ADAPTED TO

INTERIOR DECORATIONS.

WITH OBSERVATIONS ON

THE PRACTICE OF HOUSE PAINTING.

BY

D. R. HAY,

HOUSE-PAINTER AND DECORATOR TO THE QUEEN, EDINBURGH

FIRST AMERICAN,
FROM THE SIXTH LONDON EDITION.

PHILADELPHIA:
HENRY CAREY BAIRD,
INDUSTRIAL PUBLISHER,
406 Walnut Street.
1867.

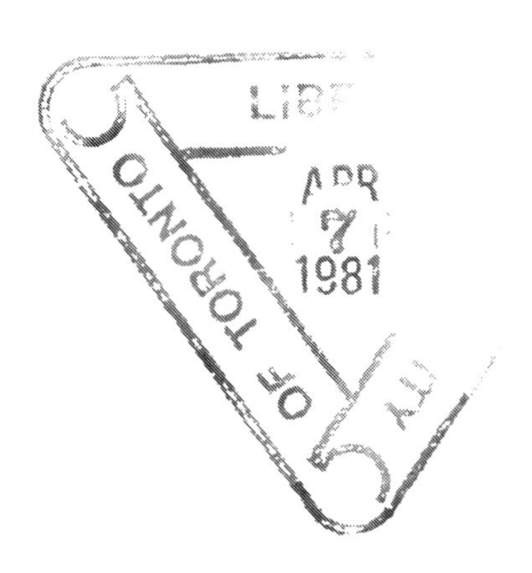

PHILADELPHIA:
COLLINS, PRINTER, 705 JAYNE STREET

PREFACE.

In laying before the public a sixth edition of this treatise, I have to express my gratitude for the favorable reception it has hitherto met with, and to assure my readers that I have thereby been stimulated to exert myself to the utmost to render it, on the present occasion, more theoretically and practically useful.

Although the colored diagrams are now reduced to one, yet that one contains all the colors of which the various diagrams in the former editions were composed, more correctly balanced as to their relative powers, and more permanently secured against change.

I have re-written the whole treatise, and have

expunged all extraneous matter in order to make room for additions more intimately connected with the subject. And as a more convenient arrangement, I have now divided it into two distinct parts; the first theoretical, and the second practical. Both of these I have treated as popularly as the nature of the subject would admit of, and, therefore, trust this edition will be found superior to any of its predecessors.

D. R. HAY.

EDINBURGH, 90 GEORGE STREET.

CONTENTS.

PART I.

PART II.

ON THE PRACTICE OF HOUSE PAINTING.

PART I.

INTRODUCTION.

Although the experimental inquiries of the natural philosopher have long since established as a scientific fact, that colors are regulated by the irrefragable laws of harmony in their combinations; and although the works of most of the masters in high art, both ancient and modern, give practical illustrations of the same truth, yet the error of considering the arrangement of various colors as a matter of mere caprice or fancy, is still prevalent.

In the decoration of our dwellings, in the colors of our dress, in the arrangement of our flower gardens, and, indeed, in almost every case where colors are brought together in the ordinary requirements of life, fashion more than scientific knowledge, seems, in a great degree, to regulate our proceedings. But the caprices of fashion are guided by no rules whatever, but are subjects upon which most nations and individuals differ widely; and there are no productions or customs to which these caprices have given rise, however extravagant or absurd, but what have had, and still have, their admirers, while they bear the gloss of novelty or stamp of fashion.

Fancy or choice is, and may be employed with perfect propriety in all matters of taste, both as to individual colors and their combinations. We are all individually entitled to have our likings for, and antipathies to particular colors, hues, shades, or tints. We may also, individually, have our partiality to particular modes of arrangement amongst various colors,—some may delight in a gay and lively style of coloring—some in the rich and powerful, and others in the deep and grave—some may have a partiality for complex arrangements, while others prefer extreme simplicity. But this is the case in music also; every variety of style and composition has its particular admirers; yet it never is assumed, that the arranging of the notes in a melody, or other musical composition, is a matter of mere caprice or fashion. All know that the arrangement of notes in such cases is regulated by fixed laws; proved also, by the experimental inquiries of the natural philosopher, to depend on certain phenomena in nature, which cannot be deviated from without giving offence to the ear; therefore, a knowledge of those laws is considered absolutely requisite to every one who wishes to cultivate that pleasing art, either practically or as an amateur. This is precisely the case in regard to coloring; for it does not matter under what circumstances a variety of colors are presented to the eye—if they be harmoniously arranged, the effect will be as agreeable to that organ as harmonious music is to the ear; but if not so arranged, the effect on the eye must be unpleasant, and the more cultivated the mind of the individual, the more annoyance will such discordance occasion him.

The laws of harmonious coloring seem not only to have been thoroughly understood by those great painters of antiquity, whose works have been the admiration and study of succeeding ages, but were even so far back as amongst the early Egyptians, carried to the greatest perfection in the more humble art of the internal and external chromatic decorations of architecture. Those travellers who have visited the remains of the magnificent cities and tombs erected by the wonderful people, speak of this branch of art as having been executed upon an evidently regular system of harmony, which had for its basis the fundamental laws, or first principles, that ought still to regulate the proceedings of the colorist, especially in those branches of art where high genius is not required, and where the practitioner must be confined within the bounds of teachable rules.

The Romans, too, at the period of their greatest refinement, seem to have paid a due regard to these laws in the applying of color to the useful arts, of which fact the remains of Pompeii and Herculaneum afford ample proof. The accounts given by artists and amateurs, of the interior decorations of the dwelling-houses of these ancient cities, all concur in eulogizing the scientific knowledge which their coloring displays. It appears, that the decorators of those days used, upon all occasions, the most brilliant and intense colors, without either discord or crudity appearing in their works. But their science did not stop here, for, by a knowledge of the various styles of coloring, and of their proper adaptation, they employed great masses of deep color, even black itself, on the walls of their rooms, sepecially such as were lighted from the top, or, rather, that were altogether uncovered; thus counteracting the brilliant and abundant light of the Italian sky. The practice of scientific coloring seems still to exist amongst the Italians. An eminent writer on the art of painting, and an amateur of the highest class,* who has done much

* James Skene, Esq, of Rubislaw.

in an official capacity for the encouragement and improvement of our national manufactures, thus describes the practice of house-painting amongst the modern Italians :—

"In Italy, the study and acquirements of a house-painter are little inferior to what is requisite for the higher branches of the art; and, in fact, the practice of both is not unfrequently combined. They are more conversant with the science, as well as the practice of coloring, with the rules of harmony, and with the composition of ornamental painting in all its branches; so that their works might be transferred to canvas, and admired for their excellence. In fact, the great frescoes of the first masters, which have been the admiration of ages, were but part of the general embellishment of the churches and palaces of Italy. And the most celebrated names in the list of artists have left memorials of their fame in the humble decorations of the arabesque, in which all the exuberance and playfulness of fancy are displayed, as well as the most enchanting harmony of brilliant colors. It is in this essential point of harmony that our practice is particularly defective; we rarely see, in the simple painting of our apartments, any combination of colors that is not in some part offensive against even the common rules of art, if there are any rules observed, save those of mere caprice or chance—although there are certain combinations pointed out by the laws of optics, which can as little be made to harmonize as two discordant notes in music. The unpleasant effects arising from such erroneous mixtures and juxtapositions, we are often sufficiently aware of, without having the skill requisite to assign the reason, any more than the painter who chose them. This accounts for the prevalent use of neutral colors in our ornamental painting, which is less liable to offend by whatever bright color it may be relieved, and likewise the safer and more agreeable combination of the different shades of the same indefinite color. But no sooner do our painters attempt any combination of decided colors than they fail The ornamental painting in Italy is almost entirely in decided colors of the most brilliant hue, and yet always inexpressibly pleasing in the combinations, because the rules of harmony are known and attended to. Neither is this proficiency confined to the decoration of palaces, or the more elaborate and expensive works; we have seen in dwellings of a much humbler cast, and indeed in general practice, the most graceful designs of ornament, painted, not in the simple manner of Camayeu, but displaying every possible tint of bold and vivid coloring, and melting into each other with all the skill and harmony of a piece of brilliant music."

Until very lately, white, neutral hues, and pale tints of color only were used in the painter's department of our internal decorations,—a practice that it is difficult at first view to account for in a country like this, where we are, by a variable climate, denied the study and enjoyment of nature's coloring for so many days in every season of the year; and must, consequently, content ourselves with what the interior decorations of our dwellings afford.

This vapid tameness in the coloring of our dwellings is the more inexcusable, when we reflect, that as harmonious music delights and refines the mind through the ear, so does harmonious coloring act as an agent of civilization, in delighting and refining the mind through the visual organ. I believe, however, that this long banishment of the true beauty of coloring from the apartments of our dwelling-houses had its origin, not in any want of feeling or taste for coloring on our part, as compared with our Continental neighbors, but from our having lost the art of applying colors harmoniously, unless by the intuitive feeling of genius. There is an inherent principle in the human mind, however uncultivated it may be, that responds to harmony—either in color, sound, or form; and as silence is preferable to bad music, so is neutrality to positive coloring, unless the latter be regulated by the laws of harmony, which render it to the eye what music is to the ear. This quality in coloring is perfectly irrespective of imitative art, for so long as the forms of the individual colors are agreeable and proportionate to the eye, so long will their harmonious arrangement convey as much pleasure to the mind, through that organ, as there is conveyed to it through the ear by the proper performance of a piece of instrumental music.

Many attribute our apathy in regard to rich coloring, to the uncongenial nature of the climate of this country. This cannot be, for in no country in the civilized world does nature exhibit, in the revolution of a year, such a splendid variety of colorific harmony—in which our snowy winter is but a pause. This pause is first interrupted by the cool vernal melody of spring, gradually leading the eye to the full rich tones of luxuriant beauty exhibited in the foliage and flowers of summer, which again as gradually rise into the more vivid and powerful harmonies of autumnal coloring, succeeded, often suddenly, by the pause of winter. But how often, in the depth of winter, when the colorless snow clothes the face of nature, do the most glorious harmonies of color present themselves in the purple and gold of a winter sky. These picturesque effects have doubtless contributed largely to distinguish the British school of painting, as a school of color. The picturesque beauty of nature's coloring, however, lies in the province of genius to imitate in works of high art; for the generality of mankind may admire it, but cannot deduce from it its first principles, in such an intelligible form, as to found laws upon them to govern that species of coloring which belongs to the more humble arts, the improvement of which is the chief object of this treatise.

What I have elsewhere said in regard to the picturesque beauty of nature's forms, I may here repeat as applicable to the no less picturesque beauty of her coloring; namely, that because it may afford the poet some of the finest themes for the exercise of his genius, we do not assume that it also supplies that knowledge of language which enables the generality of mankind to read and understand his poetry. Neither is the coloring of nature to be transferred to works of ornamental art, by means of mere imitation, any more than poetry can be produced by its mere description. The hand that blends the tints and hues in works of imitative art, must be guided by a mind so constituted, as to possess a quick and keen perception of the most subtle developments of the principles of beauty, and deeply imbued with that faculty which reciprocates at once to these developments. Such a mind constitutes that species of genius which cannot be inculcated by any process of tuition, and, therefore, none but those who possess it intuitively are capable of imitating properly the beauties of nature. To study the beauty of nature's forms and coloring, is, doubtless, one of the most delightful modes of employing the perceptive and reflective powers of the mind, but, to attempt to imitate them picturesquely, without the qualification of genius, is a waste of labor; and the adaptation of those defective imitations, indiscriminately, to ornamental purposes, has done more to degrade high art than any other species of barbarism.

For decorative purposes, and in their application to manufactures, colors must be systematized, and the elements of their various modes of combinations thoroughly understood, so that the beauty of such applications of colors could be comprehended by the generality of mankind, as easily as a simple sentence in written language. But the decorator and the manufacturer are too partial to that species of imitative art which requires the light and shade as well as the coloring of natural objects. In short, instead of acquiring a knowledge of the elementary laws of color and form, in order to apply them in the simple combinations which the humble arts of house-painting and weaving require, the poetry of high art is attempted; and, those who make the attempt not being possessed of that high genius which can reach the truth of the picturesque beauty of nature, the feelings are not touched, nor the sympathies excited by such works. It is really astonishing that people of highly cultivated minds, who can look with pleasure upon the delicate coloring and exquisite forms of the real flowers to be found in most drawing-rooms, can endure, at the same time, the sight of the wretched imitation flowers upon the paper-hangings and carpets, with which these apartments are often decorated. Habit does a great deal in familiarizing the senses to impressions that would otherwise excite very disagreeable feelings. A man with a fine ear for music may get so accustomed to the sound of sharpening saws, and the noise of the tinsmith's hammer, that in course of time they will not much annoy him. So many a person of a fine eyè for color become so accustomed to the harsh and discordant coloring of many of our carpets and paper-hangings, as to treat their presence with indifference.

Happily, there has of late years been a great movement made, in this country, towards a better knowledge of coloring in the useful arts, and especially in the decoration of our dwelling-houses. But much remains to be done, for there has as yet been little more than mere agitation, and there appears a great timidity on the part of the public generally, in respect to departing from the quiet neutrality that has so long rendered our apartments insipid and comfortless to the eye, and adopting in its stead a more full-toned and rich style of coloring.

To become acquainted with the laws of harmonious coloring—is neither a difficult nor an unpleasant task; and as the first principles upon which they are based, are identical with those upon which depend the harmony of sound and of form, their acquirement would improve our knowledge in matters of taste generally. I may here reiterate what I have on other occasions stated that in this country we are as much in want of that knowledge which conduces towards a proper appreciation of the correct and the beautiful, in works of ornamental art, as we are of operatives in that particular branch.

It would appear, however, from the recent introduction into this country of foreign artists, that our appreciation is rather gaining ground upon our practice. But although the number of those ingenious foreigners were multiplied to one hundred for each individual, it could not supersede the necessity and utility of studying those first principles to which, whether applied intuitively or through acquired knowledge, the ornamental works of these foreigners owe whatever beauty they may possess.

It is not the mere adoption of a more florid style of decoration in our public buildings, and in some of the mansions of the nobility of the land, that will do what is required to be done for this art. Every man of ordinary education ought to have such a knowledge of the teachable laws of coloring, as would enable him to be a judge of such works, and to distinguish between the affectation of harmony of color, and its true development, either by intuitive genius, or by the application of those fixed principles, a knowledge of which may be so easily acquired.

But our general knowledge, even of the propriety necessary to be observed in decoration, is so far below the requisite standard, that the grossest absurdities are often committed. For instance, we find the most flimsy and fantastical style of ornamental design, borrowed at third or fourth hand from a building devoted to the private luxury of an ancient Roman, adopted as a suitable style for the interior of an arcade, remarkable for its plain substantial massiveness, and devoted to a species of public business of such a grave nature as to be of vital importance to our prosperity and independence, as one of the nations of the civilized world. It is scarcely possible to conceive a greater degree of decorative incongruity than this, yet it has been committed in one of our greatest national edifices, amidst all the agitation that exists in regard to national advancement in the art of ornamental design.

An excellent writer on decoration in the *Athenæum*, No. 840, p. 1074, very justly observes, "That certain principles of decoration may be laid down, which, if recognized and applied, would make our dwellings much more cheerful and comfortable, which might make them comparatively beautiful, not only without any additional cost, but would make the keep of them more economical, by rendering them, to an equal degree, independent of the caprices of fashion. It is the absence of correct principles which causes decoration and furniture to be out of fashion, tiresome, palling to the eye, and subject to constant change; whereas, what is really beautiful, being based on everlasting principles, is subject to no change. We think the greater part of the painting of a house might be a work to last for a life, with benefit even to the journeymen painters, and infinite satisfaction to the house inhabitant. A truly melancholy suspension of comfort is the work of painting a house. Your whole little world so turned upside down, that it hardly rights itself before the work has to be done again. What a comfort it would be to undergo the penance only once in a life, instead of every seven years!

"It seems to us quite a mistake, though a very common and popular one, to imagine that beauty is necessarily costly in its production. Nothing could be cheaper in material and manufacture than the earthenware pots of the ancient Etrurians; yet they have perfect and everlasting beauty in their forms. The preference of one color to another, within a very wide range of colors, is not at all a thing of greater or lesser cost. So far from beauty being costly, it would more often happen, that in a given number of existing specimens of decoration, the greater beauty and harmony would be obtained at a smaller cost of labor and material, than what are expended to produce ugliness and confusion. Take at random a dozen patterns of paper-hangings, of various colors and devices, and in the majority of them, we believe it could be shown that their cost of production might be materially lessened, whilst their beauty would be greatly enhanced."

Practical experience in my profession has long

since convinced me of the correctness of these observations, and of the satisfaction and advantage arising to the employer as well as to the tradesman, by a strict adherence, on the part of the latter, to the principles here indicated.

I shall conclude this introduction by reiterating the fact—that it is to the want of an inculcation of teachable rules to the mechanic and manufacturer, as producers of beauty, and to the public generally, as appreciators of it, that we must attribute our present deficiency in Æsthetical Taste.

ON THE THEORIES OF COLOR

When I first published this Treatise there existed two theories, and I hesitated long which of the two to adopt. The one theory was that established by Sir Isaac Newton, and adopted by Sir David Brewster, and other philosohical writers on chromatics, and a short account of it may make what follows more clearly understood by the generality of readers.

The Newtonian theory was discovered, or rather the discovery of others was confirmed, by that great philosopher in the following manner:—In the window-shutter of a darkened room he made a hole of about the third of an inch in diameter, behind which, at a short distance, he placed a prism, so that a ray of the sun's light might enter, and leave it at equal angles. This ray—which before the introduction of the prism proceeded in a straight line, and formed a round spot upon a screen placed a few feet distant from the window, was now found to be refracted—appeared of an oblong form, and composed of seven different colors of the greatest brilliancy, imperceptibly blended together, viz., violet, indigo, blue, green, yellow, orange, and red. This is called the solar or prismatic spectrum.

The theory said to be established by this experiment was, that the white light of the sun is composed of several colors, which often appear by themselves, and that this white light can be separated into its elements.

By making a hole in the screen upon which the spectrum is formed, opposite to each of these colors successively, so as to allow it alone to pass, and by letting the color thus separated fall upon a second prism, Sir Isaac Newton found that the light of each of the colors was alike irrefrangible, —because the second prism could not separate any of them into an oblong image, or any other color than its own; hence, he called all the colors simple or homogeneous.

The other theory was that which seemed adopted by almost all who had written on coloring connected with the fine arts, and was, that there were only three simple or homogeneous colors, and that all others resulted from their various modes of combination. Although this theory seemed only to be established in a practical point of view, and was unsupported by any scientific experiments, yet it appeared to me more consistent with the general simplicity of nature, and I could not believe that she required seven homogeneous parts to produce what art could do by three. For instance, an artist can make all the colors, and indeed a correct representation of the prismatic spectrum (so far as the purity of his materials will allow), with three colors only, whilst, according to the theory of Sir Isaac Newton, seven simple or homogeneous colors were the constituents of the real one.

The following discovery, made by Buffon, and illustrated by succeeding philosophers, helped to strengthen me in the conviction that the scientific theory might be, like that of the practical artist, reducible to three simple or homogeneous parts. If we look steadily for a considerable time upon a spot of any given color, placed on a white or black ground, it will appear surrounded by a border of another color. And this color will uniformly be found to be that which makes up the harmonic triad of red, yellow, and blue; for if the spot be red, the border will be green, which is composed of blue and yellow; if blue, the border will be orange, composed of yellow and red; and if yellow, the border will be purple, making in all cases a triunity of the three primary colors.

With a view to throw such light upon the subject as my limited opportunities would permit, I tried over the experiments by which Sir Isaac Newton came to the conclusion, that there were seven primary elements in the solar spectrum, and the same results occurred; I could not separate any one of the colors of which it seemed composed into two. The imperceptible manner in which the colors were blended together upon the spectrum, however, and the circumstance of the colors which practical people called compound, being always found between the two of which they understood it to be composed, together with my previous conviction, induced me to continue my experiments: and although I could not, by analysis, prove that there were only three colors, I succeeded in proving it to my own satisfaction, synthetically, in the following manner:—

After having tried every color in succession, and finding that none of them could be separated into two, I next made a hole in the first screen, in the centre of the blue of the spectrum, and another in that of red. I had thereby a spot of each of these colors upon a second screen. I then, by means of another prism, directed the blue spot to the same part of the second screen on which the red appeared, where they united and produced a violet as pure and intense as that upon the spectrum. I did the same with the blue and yellow, and produced the prismatic green; as also with the red and yellow, and orange was the result. I tried, in the same manner, to mix a simple with what I thought a compound color, but they did not unite; for no sooner was the red spot thrown upon the green than it disappeared.

I tried the same experiment with two spectrums, the one behind, and of course a little above the other, and passed a spot of each color successively over the spectrum which was farthest from the window, and the same result occurred. It therefore appeared to me that these three colors had an affinity to one another that did not exist in the others, and that they could not be the same in every respect, except color and refrangibility, as had hitherto been taught.

These opinions, the result of my experiments,

I published in 1828, as being an appropriate part of a treatise of this nature, and I did so with great diffidence, well knowing that I was soaring far above my own element in making an attempt to throw light upon such a subject. I had, however, the gratification to learn that these facts were afterwards proved in a communication read to the Royal Society of Edinburgh, by Sir David Brewster, on the 21st of March, 1831, in which he showed that white light consists of the three primary colors, red, yellow, and blue; and that the other colors shown by the prism are composed of these. It may, therefore, now be confidently assumed, that there are in the scientific theory, as in that of the artist, only three primary homogeneous colors, of which all others are compounds.

It is not, however, so satisfactorily settled that the light of the sun is composed of colored rays. Transient colors are more likely to be the result of the action of light upon shade, and not the separation of light into its elements. This is not a new theory, for it was orignally advanced by Aristotle, and afterwards adopted by Leonardo da Vinci. Neither has it been set aside by modern investigators, for Göethe has taken the place of Aristotle, and it may be said that he has now established it as a fact in natural philosophy; whilst his translator, Eastlake, has, like Leonardo da Vinci, adopted and elucidated it as connected with the practice of high art.

Göethe states his opinion in the following terms:—"Light and darkness, brightness and obscurity, or, if a more general expression is preferred, light and its absence, are necessary to the production of color. Next to the light, a color appears which we call yellow, another appears next to the darkness which we call blue; when these, in their purest state, are so mixed that they are exactly equal, they produce a third color called green. Each of the two first-named colors can, however, of itself, produce a new tint, by being condensed or darkened; they thus acquire a reddish appearance, which can be increased to so great a degree that the original blue or yellow is hardly to be recognized in it; but the intensest and purest red, especially in physical cases, is produced when the two extremes of the yellow-red and the blue-red are united. This is the actual state of the appearance and generation of colors. But we can also assume an existing red in addition to the definite existing blue and yellow, and we can produce contrariwise, by mixing what we directly produce by augmentation or deepening. With these three, or six, colors, which may be conveniently included in a circle, the elementary doctrine of colors is alone concerned. All other modifications, which may be extended to infinity, have reference to the technical operations of the painter and dyer, and the various purposes of artificial life. To point out another general quality, we may observe, that colors, throughout, are to be considered as half-lights, as half shadows, on which account, if they are so mixed as reciprocally to destroy their specific hues, a shadowy tint or gray is produced."*

Eastlake observes, "That the opinion so often stated by Göethe, namely, that increase in color supposes increase of darkness, may be granted without difficulty."† Again, he observes,—"Aristotle's notion respecting the derivation of color from white and black, may perhaps be illustrated by the following opinion on the very similiar theory of Göethe. 'Göethe and Seebeck

* Göethe's *Theory of Colors.* Translated by Eastlake. Introduction, pp. xlii. xliii.

† *Ibid.* Note, p. 365.

regard color as resulting from the mixture of white and black, and ascribe to the different colors a quality of darkness (σκιερον) by the different degrees of which they are distinguished —passing from white to black, through the gradations of yellow, orange, red, violet, and blue; while green appears to be intermediate again between yellow and blue. This remark, though it has no influence in weakening the theory of colors proposed by Newton, is certainly correct, having been confirmed experimentally by the researches of Herschel, who ascertained the relative intensity of the different colored rays, by illuminating objects under the microscope by their means.

" 'Another certain proof of the difference in brightness, of the different colored rays, is afforded by the phenomena of ocular spectra. If, after gazing at the sun, the eyes are closed, so as to exclude the light, the image of the sun appears at first as a luminous or white spectrum, upon a dark ground, but it gradually passes through the series of colors to black; that is to say, until it can no longer be distinguished from the dark field of vision; and the colors which it assumes, are successively those intermediate between white and black, in the order of their illuminating power of brightness, namely, yellow, orange, red, violet, and blue. If, on the other hand, after looking for some time at the sun, we turn our eyes towards a white surface, the image of the sun is seen at first as a black spectrum upon the white surface, and gradually passes through the different colors, from the darkest to the lightest, and at last becomes white, so that it can no longer be distinguished from the white surface.' "*

These authorities appear quite sufficient to warrant the adoption of the hypothesis, that shade as well as light acts in the production of transient colors, and that the solar spectrum is the result of the ternary division of the action of light upon darkness performed by the three-sided prism.

But the original cause of light and color is a point upon which natural philosophers have not as yet come to a decision, and as little beyond conjecture had been advanced upon the subject, I hazarded the publication of an idea of my own

* *Elements of Physiology*, by J. MULLER, M D. Translated from the German by William Bailly, M. D. London. 1839.

upon it in an appendix to another work (The Nomenclature of Colors, &c.). In this hypothesis I adopted the theory, that color is an intermediate phenomenon between those of light and darkness, the perception of which, like light itself, is conveyed to the mind through the most perfect of our senses; and that the impression made upon this sense conveys to the understanding the perception of light and color, by means of some inherent quality in the atmosphere, which we know to be an elastic fluid—impenetrable, inert, movable, and possessed of a certain gravity, reducible in proportion to the degree of attenuation to which it may be subjected, and when pure, to consist principally of nitrogen gas and oxygen gas, with a small proportion of aqueous vapor and carbonic acid. Now as these elements are, according to a well-established theory, composed of individual atoms or molecules, I supposed it probable that the sun, or any other luminous body, might act upon these atomic particles, electrically or otherwise, so as to put them into harmonic motion amongst themselves, each upon its own axis, thus rendering them luminous by friction, and producing pure or white light. I supposed it also to be probable that the partial interruption of this atomic motion might produce shades,—a change in its mode, colors,—and its total interruption, blackness. As every material body is also understood to be composed of atoms, it may likewise be reasonably supposed that their modes of arrangement, in the constitution of such bodies, as well as their individual configuration, will render them capable of receiving this motion of light in ways so infinitely various, as to account for the production of every possible variety of shade and color. Many processes in dyeing produce colors simply by a change in the arrangement of the atoms of which the substance dyed is composed, thus affecting the atomic motion of light upon its surface. It is equally probable that the mode of arrangement of the atoms in crystals, and other transparent media, may be thus affected, and made to communicate a like motion to those of the atmosphere beyond them, producing colored light, as those atoms on the surface of opaque bodies reflect it.

In the article on CHROMATICS, in the *Encyclopædia Britannica*, the hypothesis advanced is, that variously colored rays emanate from the sun, each possessing a different degree of intensity, and that there may possibly be a multitude of rays of each color, moving with various velocities, and only affecting the sense when they have the velocity appropriate to that color in the eye. But the hypothesis of atomic motion which I have suggested, is independent of any such complicated process: for although the motion it supposes to be communicated by luminous bodies to the gaseous atoms may be various, the progress of the communication may be perfectly uniform.

Simplicity seems the first principle in all nature's works, and, as I have elsewhere observed, the more we investigate her operations, the more we become convinced of the simplicity of the means by which the phenomena that are daily attracting our attention are performed. If, therefore, we can account for the phenomena of light and color as satisfactorily by the means known to exist, as by supposing the necessity of material particles, or an ethereal fluid to assist these (agreeable to the different theories of Newton and Huygens), the subject is simplified, and so far agrees with the facts which philosophy has brought within the sphere of our knowledge.

ON THE ANALOGY BETWEEN COLOR AND SOUND.

HARMONIOUS arrangements of colors being such combinations as, by certain principles of our nature, produce an effect on the eye, similar to that which is produced by harmonious music on the ear, and as a remarkable conformity exists between the science of color and that of sound, in their fundamental principles, as well as in their effects, I shall probably best lead the reader to a proper comprehension of the former by tracing this analogy, the more especially as the art of music is much more generally understood, although, at the same time, it is much to be regretted that a knowledge of its first principles, or natural philosophy, is very rare, even amongst its professors. This analogy will help to show, that the laws which govern color are irrefragable, and, at the same time, a knowledge of them as practically necessary to the colorist in art, manufacture, or decoration, as a knowledge of those which govern sound is to the musician. It is well known to those who have studied music in the proper way, that there are three fundamental notes, viz., the first, third, and fifth of the scale—and technically called the tonic, the mediant, and the dominant—and that these notes, when sounded together, produce the common chord, which is the foundation of all harmony in musical composition. So it is in chromatics,—there are likewise only three fundamental colors, —blue, red, and yellow, forming the triad from which arises all harmony in painting.

By the combination of any two of these primary colors, a secondary color of a distinct kind is produced; and as only one absolutely distinct denomination of color, called a hue, can arise from a combination of the three primaries, the full number of really distinct tones is seven, corresponding to the seven notes in the complete scale of the musician. Each of these colors is capable of forming a key or tonic for an arangement, to which all the other colors introduced must refer subordinately. This reference and subordination to one particular color or hue gives a character to the whole, which is precisely the case in regard to the key-note in musical composition.

This characteristic of an arrangement of color is generally called its tone; but it appears to me that this term is more applicable to individual hues, as it is in music to voices and instruments alone. Yet, to avoid obscurity, I shall continue to use it in the sense in which it is generally applied to coloring.

From the three primary colors—yellow, red, and blue—arise, first, the secondary colors—orange, purple, and green, and then an infinite variety of hues, tints, and shades; so that the colorist, like the musician, notwithstanding the limited number of the fundamental parts of his art, has ample scope for the production of originality and beauty in the various combinations and arrangements of which they are susceptible.

The three homogeneous colors—yellow, red, and blue, have a numerical relation to each other, in their respective powers, which correspond in a remarkable manner to the numerical ratios found to exist in the respective lengths of the monochord that produce the harmonics in music, and the corresponding undulations which their vibration produce in the atmosphere.

When the three primary colors are reflected from any opaque body, in their proper proportions, neutrality is produced. They are then in an active state by reflection, but each is neutralized, to a certain extent, by the relative effect that the others have upon it. When they are absorbed, or the action which produces them interrupted, in the same proportions, they are in a passive state, and black is the result. When transmitted through any transparent body, the effect is the same; but in the first case they are material or inherent, and in the second impalpable or transient. Color, therefore, depends entirely on the reflective or refractive power of bodies, as the transmission or reflection of sound does upon their vibratory powers

The secondary colors arise from the combination of the primary colors in the following manner: Yellow and red, being mixed, produce orange color ; red and blue, purple; and yellow and blue, green; and their peculiar quality will depend upon the relative quantities and intensity of the primary colors of which they are compounded. These secondary colors are called the accidental or complimentary colors to the primaries, from the phenomenon already referred to.

And this is precisely the case in regard to musical notes. When any given note is sounded, especially upon a stringed instrument, it is either accompanied or immediately succeeded by others, which are called its harmonics. Out of this reciprocating quality amongst colors, arises all chromatic harmony, and it consequently embodies the first principles of beauty in coloring, as the harmonic relations of the three notes in music, called the tonic, the dominant, and the mediant—or the 1st, 5th, and 3d of the scale—embody the first principles of beauty in sounds. I here place the 5th before the 3d, because the numerical relation of the 5th to the 1st is relative to the number 3, whilst that of the 3d is relative to the number 5; and it is here worthy of remark, that the 5th first succeeds the tonic, although an octavo higher, and afterwards the 3d, another octavo higher. Neither do the complimentary colors appear in an intensity equivalent to the color upon which the eye rests, but evidently much weaker.

From the combination of the secondary colors arise the tertiaries or primary hues, which are also three in number, as follow: olive or blue-hue, from the mixture of the purple and green;

citron or yellow-hue, from the mixture of the green and orange; and russet or red-hue, from the mixture of orange and purple. These three colors, it will be observed, are produced by the admixture of the same ingredients — the three primaries—which always, less or more, neutralize each other in triunity. The most neutral of hues being gray, the mean between black and white, as any of the secondaries are between two of the primaries, it may appropriately be termed, although in reality a hue, the seventh color. These tertiary colors, however, stand in the same relation to the secondary colors that the secondaries do to the primaries—olive to orange, citron to purple, and russet to green; and their proportions will be found to be in the same accordance, because they neutralize each other integrally.

Out of the primary hues, by a similar mode of combination and proper balancing of their relative powers, arise the secondary hues, which have been popularly termed brown, marone, and slate, but are more properly orange-hue, purple-hue, and green-hue; and to these the same rules of contrast are equally applicable.

Besides this relation of contrast in opposition,

colors have a relation in series, which is their melody. This melody, or harmony of succession, is found in all the natural phenomena of color. Each color on the prismatic spectrum, and in the rainbow, is melodized by the two compounds which it forms with the other two primaries. For instance, the yellow is melodized by the orange on the one side, and the green on the other, the blue by the green and purple, and the red by the purple and orange. Field, in his excellent Essay on the Analogy and Harmony of Colors, has shown these coincidences by a diagram, in which he has accommodated the chromatic scale of the colorist to the diatonic series of the musician, showing that the concords and discords are also singularly coincident—but such an illustration would be too complex for a work of this simple kind.

The senses of hearing and seeing do each convey to the mind impressions of pleasure or pain, in the modes in which they are acted upon by external objects—hearing, by the modes in which such objects, by their motion, produce an effect upon the surrounding atmosphere, and seeing, by the modes in which light acts upon them. In other works I have endeavored to point out, in detail, the mathematical nature of these modes, and to show that the elements of beauty in sound, color, and form, are identical in the numerical ratios of their powers upon each other. These details need not, therefore, be gone further into here, especially as to my wish to treat the subject less abstrusely and more concisely than in the works to which reference has just been made.

Sounds, when addressed to the ear in intelligible language, convey to the mind a meaning, either descriptive of an idea, or of some object which is acknowledged by the understanding, and this may be entirely independent of music.

Forms, when intelligibly presented to the eye, representing, even in outline, any known object or established idea, convey to the mind an understanding of the object or idea entirely independent of color. It is well known as a physiological fact, that there are individuals whose ears are so constituted that they cannot distinguish music from any other species of sound, although their sense of hearing may be perfect in every other respect; and that there are also individuals whose eyes are so constituted that they are equally incapable of distinguishing colors, although their organs of vision may likewise be perfect in every other respect. Therefore, there seems to be a physiological analogy exhibited in these organs of sense.

When we reflect on the nature of music, we find it to be simply a variety of sounds, having a mathematical relation to each other in their pitch and in their duration, arranged, in the first instance, so as to follow each other in certain modes agreeably to these mathematical relations. This mode of succession produces a melody or air, which is the subject of the composition. In the second instance, that it is composed of a variety of sounds, relating also mathematically to each other in combination, or as they are made to agree with each other when produced simultaneously; and this is called harmony.

Sounds arranged in this way, convey no further intelligible meaning to the mind of man, than that which depends upon the propriety of their combination in both these respects. Now this propriety in their combination has been proved to depend upon irrefragable laws, which are based upon a branch of natural philosophy called acoustics.

The power with which the human mind may be thus affected—simply by the scientific production of sounds in successive and combined harmony, having individually in themselves no intelligible meaning—is well known. The turbid and excited mind may be soothed, and the most benign feelings of our nature excited—men may be roused from a state of apathy to attempt deeds of daring valor, or withdrawn from sinfulness to remorse and devotion—by the influence of music.

In all this we have nothing more than a scientific combination of sounds addressed to the ear. Nature also presents sounds to the ear, as she does color to the eye, in those subtle combinations that are often in both cases adopted by men of genius, as themes for the highest productions in art. From nature, we receive both impressions, with equal intensity; our eye is as much delighted by the ever varying tints and hues of the landscape, as our ear is by songs of birds, the murmuring of streamlets, or sighing of the gentle winds of summer. But in the one case, science combined with art, has enabled us to produce an infinite variety of beautiful effects, by combinations of mere sounds, while the arranging of colors, unless in connection with imitative art, is still very generally considered a matter of mere whim or caprice. Though the artist enhances his work by judicious coloring, yet it has other constituents of excellence which form its subject. In the same way, the song of the poet is enhanced by appropriate music. But the music of the composer may be produced with a certain effect, independently of the words of the poet, because the science of its composition is understood, while the coloring of the picture, for want of a knowledge of the science of chromatics, can in no other way be produced, than in connection with its language—the imitation of nature which it exhibits.

No one will deny to the eye, the power of affecting the mind as sensibly, by what it conveys to the sensorium, as the ear does through the same medium; and what is the coloring of poetry but appropriate music? and this music, as just observed, may affect the mind to a certain extent, independently of the poetry. It therefore appears clear, that if the science of coloring was properly cultivated, it might be made to affect the mind, independently of any other intelligible meaning than its scientific combination. It is such considerations as these that give importance to the analogy between color and sound. (Note A.)

ON COLORS GENERALLY.

THERE are only three distinct classes of colors, and they are termed primaries, secondaries, and tertiaries, or hues.

A PRIMARY COLOR is a simple element that cannot be separated into parts, but may be reduced to a tint by white, or to a shade by black. The admixture of either of the other two primary colors changes it to a secondary color.

A SECONDARY COLOR is consequently produced by the combination of two primary colors. These secondaries, like the primaries, may be reduced to tints and shades by the admixture of white or black, and may also, by the subordination of either of their component parts, be changed in tone, while their names generally remain the same. Hence arise an immense number of modifications of each of these secondary colors,—of orange from the yellowest to the reddest—of green from the yellowest to the bluest—and of purple from the reddest to the bluest, with a few exceptions which shall be afterwards noticed. A secondary color cannot, therefore, be changed in character, but by the admixture of its contrasting primary, or by its combination with one of the other secondaries, by either of which it becomes a hue.

A TERTIARY COLOR, or HUE, is consequently compounded of two secondary colors, and is, consequently, a mixture of the three primaries; it may, therefore, be modified in tone to a much greater extent than either of the two preceding classes. These modifications are effected by the predominance or subordination of any of its component parts, as also by the power of neutralization possessed by each of those parts upon the other two.

Each of the six colors has its specific hue, and they may be thus compounded. Yellow-hue, by orange and green; red-hue, by orange and purple; blue-hue, by purple and green; orange-hue by yellow-hue and red-hue; green-hue, by yellow-hue and blue-hue; and purple-hue by red-hue and blue-hue, as shown upon the followig diagram, a colored example of which faces the title-page.

DIAGRAM OF THE PRIMARY AND SECONDARY COLORS AND THEIR HUES.

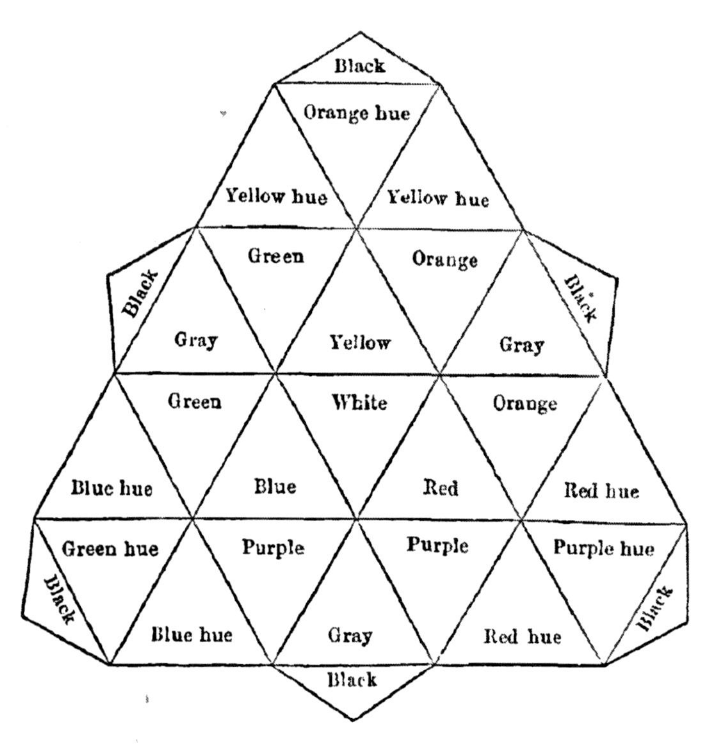

A TINT is not in itself a specific color or hue, but one of the gradations of any color or hue from its most perfect state of intensity towards white. The variety of tints is, therefore, incalculably greater than that of colors and hues.

A SHADE is, in like manner, one of the incalculable gradations of any color or hue from its most perfect state of intensity towards black.

In their contrasting powers, colors must bear relation to one another in respect to their hue, tint, and shade. A hue of any color must bear a relative proportion to the hue with which it is intended to form an equal contrast in the predominance of the color from which it takes its name. A tint of one color introduced into an arrangement as an equivalent contrast to a tint of another color, ought to be equal in diluteness, or in its stage of approximation towards white. And, in like manner, shades of two colors intended to contrast each other equally, ought to be of equal depth. All these equal contrasts depend upon the relative powers of the primary and secondary colors, one of which must predominate in every hue, tint, and shade: because when they are equally compounded, they produce neutrality. It is, therefore, easy for any one with a good eye, and such a knowledge of the relative powers of the six colors as may be very easily attained, to produce this elementary species of harmonious coloring.

Black and white, however, as they form a perfect contrast to each other, being the extremes of light and shade, impart this quality to the colors with which they are combined. Therefore, as a shade deepens towards black, the tint employed as a perfect contrast of light and shade, as well as color, ought to approximate in an equal ratio towards white.

But besides the contrasts that are equal as to color, and as to light and shade, there is a more refined species by which all the colors in a composition, except one, are held in a certain degree of subordination, in order to give that particular color a force or prominence in the group; and this applies to the light and shade by which the intensity of the colors is reduced, as much as to the colors themselves. Such contrasts may be termed imperfect, and it is by these especially that the teachable coloring of the decorator or of the manufacturer, can approach the unteachable coloring of high art. As a knowledge of these contrasts can only be given by going into greater detail than would be consistent with the simple nature of this treatise,—and, indeed, could not be understood without such a number of colored diagrams as would render it too expensive for many of those for whose use it is principally intended,—I must refer such of my readers as may wish to go more deeply into the subject, to my "Principles of Beauty in Coloring Systematized," and my "Nomenclature of Colors, Hues, Tints, and Shades."

As the effect of all arrangements of colors depends as much on the media which accompany and unite them as on the colors themselves, the greatest attention ought to be paid to the tone and character of this class of hues. It is by adapting them properly that the greatest distinctions are reconciled and brought to an imperceptible adjunct; and it is by them that tone, keeping, and repose, are given to the whole. A neglect of these mediatory colors is the chief cause of that crudity and confusion of parts, so conspicuous in many of the colored goods manufactured at the present period.

In arranging colors, therefore, either in manufactures or decoration, whether a few or a great variety are to be employed, the effect of the whole, as well as the several component parts, will depend as much on attention to this as on the skill with which they are harmonized in contrast and succession to each other. And it must be borne in mind, that no perfectly harmonious arrangement of colors can be made unless all the three primaries be present, either in a simple or mixed state; and that the distinctions of harmony depend upon a predominance, either of one of these three, or of one of the secondaries.

The diagram to which I have already alluded, exhibits a general harmony of all the colors of any distinctive character, simple and compound, except the neutral gray, which is represented, although imperfectly, by the engraved groundwork. It will be observed that each limb of this diagram forms a series of hues proceeding from one of the primaries, and producing a distinct melody, or harmony in succession, of that color. It will also be seen, that in each of these harmonies, although a primary color predominates, as a key-note does in music, the other two primaries enter, in combination, into the arrangement, as shall be more fully noticed in treating of them separately. There is also shown, upon this diagram, the progress of color from light to darkness, or from white to black; as also in its nine central divisions, the harmony, in succession and contrast, of the primary and secondary colors. Its general arrangement, I trust, will likewise show that all the colors and hues, in their greatest intensity, may be brought together without crudity or harshness resulting from their combination.

The terms warm and cold, as applied to color, are not very generally understood; I shall, therefore, endeavor to explain their meaning. Of the three primary colors, red is most allied to warmth, and blue to coldness, whilst yellow remains neutral in these respects. Indeed, red fully embodies the principle of warmth, and blue of coldness, because wherever the former predominates in any mixed color, the tone is reckoned warm in the degree of such predominance; and where the latter predominates, the compound is termed a cool-toned hue, to the extent also of the predominance of that color. The term warm, or hot, as some writers have it, being applied to red, in art, may have originated in the resemblance of that color to fire, as much as from its powerful effect upon the eye; and that of cold, to blue, from being so opposite to red in its effects; but, whatever the terms may have arisen from, they are perfectly significant, and thoroughly understood by painters and amateurs. It should, therefore, be kept in view, that yellow is a color allied to light, without being either of a cool or a warm tone—that red is intermediate as to light and shade, but decidedly of a warm tone—and that blue is a color allied to darkness, and decidedly of a cool tone. Red is not altered in tone by the introduction of yellow, because the product of the mixture, orange, is decidedly a warm-toned color; neither is blue altered in tone by the introduction of yellow, because the product of the mixture, green, is a cool-toned color. Yellow imparts light to red and blue, and blue imparts shade to red and yellow.

In all general arrangements, which are not necessarily confined to any particular leading color, it ought to be kept in view, what nature has pointed out in the most distinct manner in all her coloring, namely, that those cool-toned and tempered colors which are most agreeable to the eye should predominate, and that vivid and intense colors should upon all occasions be used with a sparing hand.

ON THE APPLICATION OF THE LAWS OF HARMONIOUS COLORING TO HOUSE-PAINTING AND MANUFACTURES.

The house-painter should start with the principle so apparent in the coloring of nature, to which reference has just been made, namely, that bright and intense colors should be used with a sparing hand, especially in situations where they receive a direct light; and that such colors should only be employed to heighten the general effect, and to add splendor to rich and full-toned arrangements by their sparkling qualities.

The manufacturer has a greater latitude, for his productions may, in most cases, be neutralized by what accompanies them in a more general arrangement. In the finest specimens of Persian and Turkish carpets, the deep tones of indigo and brown predominate, while the bright hues and tints only appear to detail and heighten the effect of the pattern.

It has been said that coloring, like sound in music or poetry, should be an echo to the sense, and according to the general sentiment which the subject should inspire, it will be gay, lively, sombre, or solemn. Although this remark was made with reference to subjects of high art, it is equally applicable to the coloring of the apartments of a dwelling-house, and, indeed, to that of every building whatever, as well as to every kind of colored manufacture employed in their decoration.

Every artist in the higher branches of painting has a particular style of coloring to study, peculiarly adapted to the nature of the generality of his subjects, but the house-painter's styles must not only be as various as the uses of the apartments which he decorates, but must vary according to the different tastes of his employers: and, further, he must take into consideration not only the style of architecture, the situation, whether in town or country, but the very rays by which each apartment is lighted, whether they proceed directly from the sun, or are merely reflected from the northern sky; he must confine himself to neither a vivid, sombre, warm, nor cold style of coloring; all must be equally at his command, and in all, the same strict attention to harmony must be observed.

The house-painter has often another very serious difficulty to encounter. A variety of highly and variously-colored furniture is shown him, to which the coloring of the different parts of a room must be suited; it is here that his powers of balancing, harmonizing, and uniting, are called forth; it is this which obliges him, as Sir Joshua Reynolds says of the artist, ever to hold a balance in his hand, by which he must decide the value of different qualities, that, when some fault *must* be committed, he may choose the least.

In toning and harmonizing the colors in a picture, an artist has the assistance of light and shadow, and can make his shades accord with the tone in such a manner as to improve the general harmony; but as the colors of the house-painter and manufacturer are all liable to be placed in full light, they must be toned in themselves, to prevent that unnatural crudeness so annoying to the eye. How, then, can we account for the continued prevalence of those gaudy paper-hangings which impinge the most powerful rays in all their vigor, or those carpets where the preponderance of bright yellow and red attracts the eye, and injures the effect of everything which is placed upon them? And if, according to the rules which regulate the higher branches of the art, simplicity of arrangement prevents confusion, where a variety of colors are introduced, the colors, on the generality of such articles, are most erroneously arranged. These errors must proceed from a general negligence of the rules of harmony. I do not mean by this that bright and vivid colors are always offensive. I have already said that they add richness and grandeur, when used in their proper places, and in proper quantities; but they should by no means cover the floor or walls of an apartment, unless under very peculiar circumstances. It may here be observed, that in all pictures representing interiors, when a group of figures is introduced, there may occasionally appear a piece of rich drapery or furniture, painted in equally vivid and bright colors with the figures, and which may, in a great measure, improve the general effect and harmony; but who ever saw, in a work of merit, the colors on the wall, or carpet on the floor of the apartment, making a monopoly of attraction, and causing those upon the figures and furniture to sink into insignificance?

There may be many excellences in a picture which may compensate for a defect in harmony, and the artist may still retain a high character for drawing, expression, &c.; but nothing can excuse a deficiency in this respect either in an apartment or a piece of manufacture. If the decorations of the apartment or fabric of the cloth be costly, the defect in harmony is the more to be regretted.

I have asserted that a want of knowledge, or general neglgence of the rules in harmony, is the cause of our errors in decoration and manufactures; and this fact is still apparent, even in regard to our most splendid habitations and palaces, the apartments in which, although often rendered pleasing from the interest excited by the profusion of pictures with which they are hung, too often display a want of harmony in their other decorations. This does not always proceed from the painting alone, but often from a want of unison between it and the furniture; for each may be perfect in its own way, and yet the harshest discord exist between them.

This is an obvious defect; for when there is no particular tone or key fixed on for the coloring of an apartment,—that is, when one part of the furniture is chosen without any reference to the rest, and the painting done without any reference to the furniture, discord is generally the result. Such an incongruous mixture is, in comparison to a tastefully decorated apartment, as far as regards coloring, what a child produces with its first box of paints to a good picture.

A second and more common fault is the predominance of some bright and intense color, either upon the walls or floor. It is evident that the predominance of a bright and overpowering color upon so large a space as the floor or wall of a room, must injure the effect of the finest furniture.

This great error often arises from the difficulty of choosing a paper-hanging or carpet, and our liability to be bewildered amongst the multitude of patterns which are produced, the most attractive of which, on a small scale, are often, from this very circumstance, the more objectionable in regard to their forming a large mass in an apartment; particularly as the artists who design them seem to be regulated by no fixed principles, but, from their repeated deviations from the established rules of harmony, appear to give themselves up to the vague pursuit of novelty alone.

A third error is introducing deep and pale colors, which may have been well enough chosen in regard to their hues, but whose particular degrees of strength or tint have not been attended to. Thus the intensity of one or more may so affect those which they were intended to balance and relieve as to give them a faded and unfinished appearance. This may proceed from applying the general laws without any regard to the more subtle principles of the art; for, although it is always necessary to subdue and temper such colors as are introduced in large quantities, yet when they are reduced by dilution alone the effect cannot be good. This error is also very common in the coloring of carpets and paper-hangings. In such productions the degree of intensity of the individual colors is seldom taken into account. A pale tint of blue is often introduced as an equivalent to the richest orange color, and sometimes a small portion of lilac—one of the lightest tints of purple—as a balancing color to a quantity of the most intense yellow. This is inverting the natural order of colors altogether, as will be more particularly shown in the sequel.

There is a fourth defect, and rather a common one, and that is, a want of the media already alluded to, as uniting and harmonizing an assemblage of bright colors, which may, in other respects, be perfectly well arranged; for it is a rule in the higher branches of the art, that confusion of parts of equal strength should always be avoided. A room of this description resembles a Chinese landscape, where foreground and distance are unceremoniously jumbled together.

An opposite defect to this has already been referred to,—namely, monotony, or a total want of variety; for some are so afraid of committing errors in point of harmony, that neutral tints only are introduced, and sometimes one tint of this kind alone prevails. Variety is a quality found to exist in the most trifling as well as in the grandest combinations of nature's coloring; and it is, as already observed, in uniting and making an arrangement of various colors harmonious and agreeable to the eye, that the skill of the house-painter and manufacturer chiefly consists. It is this which produces what is termed repose in a picture, a quality equally desirable in the coloring of an apartment.

The foregoing observations have been fully borne out by subsequent writers on this art. The writer in the *Athenæum*, already quoted, observes:—

"For our part, we are disposed to believe harmonious coloring, consistently employed in the decoration of all buildings—inhabited buildings especially, where we spend a great part of our lives—not to be either slight or unimportant in its influence on the moral tone of the inhabitants. As we may read to some extent the character of individuals in their dress, so we believe we might do so, in the character of their dwellings. Hence a very dull-minded, tasteless people we may be pronounced to have been during the eighteenth century. A room of bright and cheerful appearance surely tends to dispel gloomy and melancholy associations, whilst a dark and dismal cell provokes them. Glitter and tawdriness disturb thoughtfulness, whilst quietude in coloring tends to suggest it.

"'Experience,' says Göethe, 'teaches us that particular colors excite particular states of feeling.' It is related of a witty Frenchman, 'Il pretendoit que son ton de conversation avec Madame étoit changé depuis qu'elle avoit changé en cramoisi le meuble de son cabinet, qui étoit bleu.'

"The great majority of domestic apartments at the present time, even in houses of the first class, have scarcely any marked feature of decoration about them which indicates taste or knowledge. They present a monotonous sameness and deficiency of any principles of taste—the varieties of character which occur, from time to time, being regulated only by the caprices of fashion. Sometimes every room you enter is of one color. In one of the most splendid of modern houses in the metropolis—we mean in Sutherland House—we have been especially struck with the monotony of white and profuse gilding, in the forms of the Louis Quinze period. Sometimes the rage is for warm shades of coloring, at others for cold, though the preponderating taste seems to take refuge in dull, characterless, neutral coloring. 'People of refinement (to quote Göethe again) 'have a disinclination to colors. This may be owing partly to weakness of sight, partly to the uncertainty of taste, which readily takes refuge in absolute negation.' During one season salmon color, as it is called, reigns supreme; then sage color succeeds salmon; drab follows sage or slate; and then all varieties of crimson put out the drabs. Each is employed in its turn, without the slightest reference to any of the questions which should determine its appropriateness or otherwise. It is the same with ornamental patterns. One year you find every drawing-room papered with patterns of flowers, another year scrolls will be all the rage. One year small patterns are correct—in the following, large only can be tolerated; and whilst each fashion reigned, each was exclusively used. Crimson walls in south aspects, leaden-colored ones in north aspects. Small patterns applied to rooms large and small, and large patterns to rooms small and large. A like absence of any recognized principle is seen in the carpets and hangings. When crimson walls were oftenest seen, then was the call for drab and light-colored carpets. More by luck than anything else, it is now the fashion to have the carpets darker in color than the walls. We may often enter a room which, preserving something of each shifting fashion of the few past years, exhibits a violation of every principle of harmonious decoration. Walls of a hot and positive color in a room with a southern aspect—blue ceilings fuller of color than the drab carpets, with curtains and hangings of scarlet—and perchance a huge sofa covered with black horse-hair. Not a single thing appropriate or consistent, but the whole a medley of unsuitableness."

To proceed properly in decoration, the tone or key is the first point to be fixed, and its degree of warmth or coldness will be regulated by the use, aspect, and light of the apartment. The next point is the style of coloring—whether gay, sombre, or otherwise. This is more particularly regulated by the use of the apartment, and the sentiments which it ought to inspire; for, as Sir Joshua Reynolds says, in regard to coloring, "What may heighten the elegant may degrade the sublime." Unison, or a proper combination of parts, is the next consideration.

The tone is generally fixed by the choice of the furniture, and this ought to have particular reference to the aspect, because the furniture of a room may be considered, in regard to coloring, in the same light as a key-note in music, or as the principal figures in a picture, and the general tone must, therefore, depend upon the colors of which it is composed; for instance, if the pre-vailing color be blue, gray, cool green, or lilac, the general tone must be cool; but if, on the other hand, it be red, orange, brown, yellow, or a warm tint of green, the tone must be warm. But, as stated before, there can be no pleasing combination of colors without variety. This, by judicious management, may be given without in the least interfering with the tone, for it is merely the general color of the furniture which ought to fix the tone, and there may be the most decided contrasts in its parts, which, by the introduction of proper medial hues throughout the room, can be reconciled and united. Apartments lighted from the south and west, particularly in a summer residence, should be cool in their coloring; but the apartments of a town house ought all to approach towards a warm tone, as also such apartments as are lighted from the north and east of a country residence.

When the tone of an apartment is therefore fixed, first by the aspect and then by the choice of the furniture, it is the business of the house-painter to introduce such tints upon the ceiling, walls, and wood-work as will unite the whole in perfect harmony. This, as I have already observed, is a difficult task: the colors of the furniture may be arranged by a general knowledge of the laws of harmony, but the painter's part cannot be properly added without the closest attention to the more subtle operations of those laws.

The style of coloring is the next point to be fixed, and will depend entirely on the use of the apartment. In a drawing-room, vivacity, gayety, and light cheerfulness, should characterize the coloring. This is produced by the introduction of tints of brilliant colors, with a considerable degree of contrast and gliding; but the brightest colors and strongest contrasts should be upon the furniture, the effect of which will derive additional value and brilliancy from the walls being kept in due subordination, although, at the same time, partaking of the general liveliness.

The characteristic coloring of a dining-room should be warm, rich, and substantial; and where contrasts are introduced, they should not be vivid. This style of coloring will be found to correspond best with the massive description of the furniture: gilding, unless in very small quantities for the sake of relief, or to carry off the effect of picture-frames, should be avoided.

Breakfast parlors ought to be painted in a

medial style between that of a drawing-room and dining-room.

The most appropriate style of coloring for libraries is rich and grave, and no higher coloring should be employed than is necessary to give the effect of grandeur, and unite the painting with the richness produced by the bookbinder's art. This can scarcely be done by neutral hues; but care should be taken not to disturb the quietness which ought to characterize the coloring of all apartments of this description by any masses of vivid color.

In bed-rooms, a light, cleanly, and cheerful style of coloring is the most appropriate. A greater degree of contrast may be here admitted between the room and its furniture than in any other apartment, as the bed and window-curtains form a sufficient mass to balance a tint of equal intensity upon the walls. There may, also, for the same reason, be admitted gayer and brighter colors upon the carpet.

Staircases, lobbies, and vestibules, should all be rather of a cool tone, and the style of the color should be simple and free of contrast. The effect to be produced is that of architectural grandeur, which owes its beauty more to the effect of light and shadow than to any arrangement of colors; yet they ought not to be so entirely free from color as the exterior of a mansion, but should be in coloring what they are in use—a link between exterior simplicity and interior richness.

Staircases and lobbies being made cool in tone, and simple in the style of their coloring, will much improve the effect of the apartments which enter from them.

It will be observed, that in the foregoing observations I have taken notice only of such apartments as are to be found in the town or country residences of gentlemen of modern fortune; and, although, the general principles I have endeavored to elucidate are equally applicable to the palace and the cottage, yet, in the higher class of edifices, we find grand staircases, corridors, saloons, &c., requiring in every individual case a peculiar mode of treatment, for which it is impossible to lay down any general rules.

ON COLORS INDIVIDUALLY.

WHITE is the full and unmodified action of that atomic motion which is, agreeably to the hypothesis already explained, assumed to be the cause of light being reflected from the surface of bodies, as black is understood to be the total interruption of that motion. White is therefore naturally contrasted by black. The first modification of this atomic motion that has a distinctive character, as a primary element in the chromatic series, is that which produces yellow—a less vigorous action—because the presence of color implies shade, and shade is a modification of light towards darkness. Yellow is, therefore, the melodizing color to white in the primary series. White harmonizes in conjunction and opposition with all colors. In conjunction, it produces every variety of tint, and in opposition, it contrasts in various degrees of power, in proportion as the principle of shade or of color is opposed to it. For instance, when opposed to blue, the contrast is less powerful than that produced by its opposition to black, but more pleasing, because the coldness of the blue thus imparts a warmth of tone to the white, however colorless it may have appeared previously to its being placed in juxtaposition with the blue. In like manner, white appears of a cool tone when contrasted with red, but pure yellow, from being its melodizing color, does not affect its tone by contrast. White, from being the representative of light, has a gay and cheerful effect upon the eye.

Popularly, there are various kinds of white—under the names, cream-white, French-white, pearl-white—and even the terms reddish-white and bluish-white are sometimes used. But this is a false nomenclature, for all those whites are tints of specific colors, and they ought to be named as such. Cream-white, for instance, is a light tint of yellowish orange-color; French-white—a light tint of reddish purple; and pearl-white—a light tint of bluish purple. When a light tint of any color is placed beside the color itself in an intense state, the tint will certainly appear a pure white, but if placed against pure white, the color with which it is tinged will appear, and it is, therefore, a tint of that color. Having, however, elsewhere entered into the subject of *nomenclature* fully, and wishing to retain the original simplicity of this treatise as much as possible, I shall continue, in this Part, the same nomenclature adopted in the former editions.

French-white and cream-white are the only two whites which are generally understood, or used in decorations besides the purest white. The first of these being of all tints the most aerial, is often employed in house-painting, and when the situation, furnishing, and character of an apartment are properly adapted, it has an extremely pleasing effect. Either French-white, or cream-white, may be made the prevailing color of a drawing-room in a country residence, and where the hangings and furniture are composed of light blue, or any other delicate tint of silk, satin-wood, various light marbles, and gilding, the most lively and cheerful effect imaginable is produced. It may be requisite to observe, that French-white, when used on walls, should be kept rather low in tone, so as not to interfere with the effect of the furniture. This peculiar tint can only be introduced when all the other tints are light and cool in tone, as any quantity of intense or rich coloring completely subdues it; and where gilding forms part of the arrangement, a little additional warmth should be given to its tone. The same may be said of pure white—all colors brought into contact with it should be light and cool, amongst which tints of gray and green are the most suitable. Very light yellow, of the tint of the primrose, forms also a pleasing melody with pure white.

In rooms where white and other cool tints predominate upon the walls and wood-work, the furniture should be of an equally light description. Bamboo and satin-wood are the best woods. The same considerations should regulate the choice of the carpet and curtains. White, not many years ago, was the only color in use for the wood-work of rooms of every description: it has now almost entirely given way to shades of various colors, and imitations of the finer kinds of woods. It is still, however, adopted for bed-rooms, particularly in summer residences, where its light, cheerful, and cleanly effect is extremely pleasing, when not destroyed by the introduction of strong and deep colors.

A south light is the best for white, and all such colors and furniture as assimilate to it. When it is the predominating color in a room lighted from the north, it ought to approach slightly towards a cream-color, so as to counteract as much as possible the cold reflection of such a light.

In patterns for colored manufactures, pure white ought not to be used along with intense and rich colors, unless melodized by light and delicate tints Indeed, it ought, in manufactures as in decoration, only to be used where the character of the arrangement is of a light and delicate nature. Its effect in arrangements of deep, rich, and intense colors, is generally harsh and spotty. When employed as a groundwork for a carpet, it ought to be, to a certain extent, reduced in intensity, by which great additional effect will be given to the tints with which the pattern is colored. When the general tone of a pattern of this description is warm,—that is, where red and yellow prevail, the white ought to be slightly tinged towards a cream-color. On the other hand, when the tone is cool, blue or green being the prevailing color, it may be tinged towards purple or gray. When white, however, is used, not as the medium to an arrangement, but as a contrasting color to any particular tint, it ought to be toned with the opposite hue.

YELLOW, of the three primaries, partakes most of the nature of white, being the lightest of all decided colors, and the brightest on the prismatic spectrum: it is neither a warm nor a cold color. Its contrasting color is purple, a compound of the other two primaries. It combines with red in producing orange-color, and when compounded with blue, it produces green. These are, therefore, its melodizing colors. It is the most powerful of the positive colors as to light, and consequently the least agreeable to the eye when unaccompanied, or when predominating in a pure state. Being the most allied to light of the positive colors, it, next to white, forms the most powerful contrast to black. There are many varieties of yellow in the popular nomenclature of colors: but what is here meant by yellow is the color of the yellow jasmyn, or most intense lemon color. Yellow, of course, forms a component part of all the tertiary or neutral hues, either in predominance or subordination.

The tertiary in which it is the archeus or ruling color is that commonly called citron, but more properly yellow-hue, which being a compound of orange and green, the two secondaries into which yellow enters, has a greater proportion of that color than either of the other two tertiaries. Citron, or yellow-hue, is of itself a soft and pleasing color to the eye, and is the lightest of all the distinct hues arising out of the treble combination of the primaries. It is very useful as a contrasting color amongst low tones of purple and crimson. In tracing yellow still further down in the scale, the next understood color in which it predominates is the semi-neutral hue, brown, or orange-hue—a most efficient color in all the low parts of every warm-toned arrangement.

The upper limb of the colored diagram which faces the title-page exhibits yellow in its various combinations and gradations of hue down to black. There are, of course, countless intermediate hues and shades between any two of those upon the diagram.

In artificial lights, pure yellow apparently

loses much of its intensity, because it cannot be easily distinguished from white. This occurs from all such lights being less or more of a yellow tone, and consequently, diffusing this color over all objects within their influence: white thereby becoming yellow, and yellow remaining unaltered.

In decoration, pure yellow cannot be employed in large masses, but merely as a heightening color; yet light tints of yellow have a very pleasing effect in bedrooms, especially such as are lighted from the north and east, and form an agreeable arrangement with white, lilac, or chintz furniture. They have also the advantage of being easily lighted, and thereby appearing very cheerful at night.

There is no color that requires more management than yellow in colored manufactures, yet in these it is almost always employed in its purest and brightest tones: while the other colors, which, according to their relative powers, ought to be of greater intensity, are very generally much weaker. Whether this proceeds from the ease with which it is produced in dyeing, or from a desire to produce a striking effect, it is hard to say, but its abuse in this way must be apparent to all people of taste who have paid any attention to the matter. Yellow is, however, in its various tints and combinations, of the greatest value in producing brilliancy and richness, as will be afterwards shown.

Some of Goethe's remarks upon yellow, and some of the colors that proceed from it, are curious. He says: "When a yellow color is communicated to dull and coarse surfaces, such as common cloth, felt, or the like, on which it does not appear with full energy, the disagreeable effect is apparent. By a slight and scarcely perceptible change, the beautiful impression of fire and gold is transformed into one not undeserving the epithet foul, and the color of harmony and joy reversed to that of ignominy and aversion. To this impression the yellow hats of bankrupts, and the yellow circles on the mantles of Jews, may have owed their origin. As no color can be considered as stationary, so we can very easily augment yellow into reddish by condensing or darkening it. The color increases in energy, and appears in red-yellow more powerful and splendid All that we have said of yellow is applicable here in a higher degree. The red-yellow gives an impression of warmth and gladness, since it represents the hue of the intense glow of fire, and of the milder radiance of the setting sun. Hence it is agreeable around us; and again, as clothing, in greater or less degrees is cheerful and magnificent. A slight tendency to red immediately gives a new character to yellow; and while the English and Germans content themselves with pale-yellow colors in leather, the French, as Costel has remarked, prefer a yellow enhanced to red; indeed, in general, everything in color is agreeable which belongs to the active side. As a pure yellow passes very easily to red-yellow, so the deepening of this last to yellow-red is not to be arrested. The agreeable, cheerful sensation which red-yellow excites, increases to an intolerably painful impression in bright yellow-red. The active side is here in its highest energy; and it is not to be wondered at that impetuous, robust, uneducated men should be especially pleased with this color. Among savage nations the inclination for it has been universally remarked; and when children, left to themselves, begin to use tints, they never spare vermilion and minium. In looking steadfastly at a perfectly yellow-red surface, the color seems actually to penetrate the organ. It produces an extreme excitement, and still acts thus when somewhat darkened. A yellow-red cloth disturbs and enrages animals. I have known men of education to whom its effect was intolerable, if they chanced to see a person dressed in a scarlet cloak, on a gray, cloudy day." *

It will here be observed that Göethe terms what we call orange-color, red-yellow, and what we call scarlet, yellow-red, which is, certainly, a more correct nomenclature.

ORANGE-COLOR is the next color in the series; it is a compound of yellow and red, in equal proportions. Between these two colors it appears in the prismatic spectrum, rainbow, and other natural phenomena; they may, therefore, be termed its melodizing colors. Its contrasting color is blue. Orange-color is the extreme point of warmth in coloring; because the red, in which exists the principle of warmth, is lighted up by a color whose nature does not reduce this warmth, but, by adding light to it, gives it more intensity. Therefore, as blue embodies the principle of coldness of tone, and has least light of any decided color, the contrast between orange and blue is more powerful than that between any other two colors. In its combination with green, orange produces the tertiary citron, and with purple the tertiary russet.

Although orange-color is perhaps the most powerful of all colors, yet it possesses a mellowness and richness which renders it one of the most effective in all general arrangements. It should, however, next to yellow, be employed with a very sparing hand; for it is, as well as that primary and red, offensive to the eye when viewed alone, and unresolved by a proper proportion of its contrasting and melodizing colors and hues. The various beautiful tints produced by the dilution of orange are the most useful in heightening all ornamental coloring, amongst which that termed gold-color is pre-eminent. Orange-color, like the other two secondaries, has great variety of hue, according to the predominance of either of its component parts. As it advances towards yellow, by a predominance of that color in its mixture, pure blue can no longer be employed as a perfect contrast or neutralizing color, but hues of purple, advancing towards the perfect state of that color in the same ratio as the orange-color advances towards yellow.

On the other hand, when orange-color recedes towards red, by a subordination of yellow in its composition, green, in its various hues, becomes the perfect contrasting color; and as the red predominates in the orange-color, so ought the green to approach towards its perfect or prismatic purity. It is not, however, always necessary or desirable that colors employed as harmonizing accompaniments to one another should be of equal power, although it is most essential to the colorist to know the proper method of making them so.

Suppose orange-color to be the key adopted for an arrangement of colors, either in the decoration of an apartment, or in the design of a carpet, or other piece of manufacture, the blue ought to be subordinate, either in intensity or quantity; and this subordination in intensity ought to be in shade rather than tint, or by neutralizing the blue by the admixture of a small portion of orange-color.

In the medial colors employed in an arrangement of this character, the deep rich tones of russet, citron, and brown, or, more properly, red-hue, yellow-hue, and orange-hue, ought to predominate, relieved occasionally by the deepest shades of indigo or deep purplish blue. Black and white are both out of tone in such an arrangement, especially the latter.

Pure orange-color, from its great power, is not often employed in decoration, yet many of its hues are the best adapted for window-curtains, chair seats, and other furniture, where gorgeousness and splendor are desirable. The gold and giraffe hues so employed, along with pure emerald-green on the walls, produce when properly harmonized by their accompaniments, one of the most pleasing effects in ordinary decoration. In this case, however, the green is the ruling color, and such an arrangement will therefore admit of all such hues, shades, and tints being introduced as harmonize with that color.

RED is the third in the chromatic series, and second of the primaries. It is the most positive of all colors; holding the middle station between yellow, which is most allied to light, and blue, which is most allied to shade—it is of all colors the most powerful. The secondaries with which it melodizes in series are, of course, orange and purple, which are produced by its combinations with the other two primaries. Its contrasting color is green, a compound of yellow and blue, in equal portions as to power. Red is decidedly a warm color, and, to a certain extent, communicates this quality to every color or hue into which it enters.

The effect of warmth is most apparent in its combinations with yellow, for in those with blue it becomes more cool and retiring. From the medial situation of red, and from its power in subduing the effect of such colors as enter, in minute proportion, into combination with it, its name is very indiscriminately applied. The first decided or specific color produced in its approach towards yellow is scarlet, called by Goethe yellow-red, and in its approach towards purple it produces the most splendid of all its various tones—crimson. But before arriving at either of these understood colors, there are an immense variety of tones, to all of which the general term red is commonly applied. It is not easy to describe what is meant by pure red; probably the most intense geranium-color is the nearest approximation generally understood. That which I have given upon the diagram is the nearest I could produce by a pigment, yet it is far from being perfect.

The tertiary in which red predominates is russet, or red-hue, a medial hue between purple and orange, and consequently having a double occurrence of red in its composition; therefore, it is the most positive and warm of the hues. It is of great power and value in all the deep parts of any warm-toned arrangement, as a contrasting color to the deep hues of green, necessarily brought in as relieving colors. The semi-neutral marone, or purple-hue, is the next understood hue in its descent to black. This hue is the most useful of all semi-neutrals in such arrangements as are best adapted for patterns of carpets, and other variously colored manufactures. It is deep and clear, and although allied to red, is sufficiently cool to admit of its being used as the deepest shade in such arrangements as have a predominance of cool-toned colors.

From the positive nature of red, there is no color that requires more toning and management, when exhibited in large masses, either in decoration or in variously colored manufacture. The effect of red individually being striking and powerful, it has, like yellow, been much too indiscriminately employed. We have only to look at nature for the proper use of this color.

We shall there see that red seldom appears in its full intensity, and when it does so, it is at that season when its effect is balanced and neutralized by the general verdure which clothes the earth. Red, however, in nature as in art, is indispensable in producing, by combination, that variety of hue so essential to the effect of every arrangement of colors. The landscape painter knows well that neither sky, water, nor foliage, can be successfully imitated without the introduction of this color.

Pure red, and its various approximations towards scarlet, are too violent and obstrusive to be used in large masses, either in decoration or in any general arrangements of colors upon a piece of manufacture, unless under very peculiar circumstances. It forms, however, like orange, an excellent leading color or key-note. On all such occasions, its contrasting color, green, ought to be tempered by being toned towards olive: bright green, if employed at all, ought to be used in very small quantities. The tertiaries ought generally to be those in which red predominates, and blue is subordinate to yellow, and these should be relieved by deep rich hues of green.

A small proportion of gold-color adds brilliancy and effect to arrangements of this description.

There is an exception, however, to this rule in decoration; some rooms are so lighted that the direct rays are entirely thrown upon the floor, and the walls left comparatively in shade. In cases of this kind, I have known a bright scarlet upon the wall produce an excellent effect, the want of direct light preventing it from obtruding upon the eye. In such cases deep-toned colors ought to predominate on the carpet. Gilding is of much importance in melodizing and heightening the effect of apartments decorated in this style.

Crimson is, of all the tones arising from the mellowing of the primary red, the most gorgeous and useful as a leading color. The green which relieves it best is that which approaches the citron hue. This color, from the splendid and rich effect which it always produces, and from its being, of all the tones of red, the most cool and mellow, is much used in internal decoration. It is also, when of a proper shade and tone, an excellent ground for pictures, and associates well with gilding. This latter quality proceeds from the crimson partaking, in a small degree, of the property of purple as well as red—the one being the contrasting color to yellow, and the other the melodizing color to orange; the color of gold, in its lights and shadows, producing these two.

From these circumstances, crimson, of a proper depth and hue, has been generally adopted as a ground for pictures, by the proprietors of those splendid mansions where the finest collections are to be seen. This has led to its adoption in general; but, from the great variety of hues which are produced under this name, many glaring errors have arisen. Most of the flocked papers so much in use, and erroneously called crimson, partake more of the tone of scarlet, while others are crimson on the pattern, with a tint of pink on the ground. This often arises from the pattern being of one material and the ground of another; and even when the ground and pattern are at first the same, the former from its being a thin wash of water-color upon white paper, is soon reduced to a pale pink—while the pattern, from its facility in collecting dust, becomes a dark sombre red.

From crimson proceeds that beautiful series of tints called pinks or rose colors, which are so essential as heightening reds in all cool-toned arrangements.

There are various other denominations of red, but they are all, with the exception of the purest color, compounds of two or all of the primaries.

PURPLE lies next in series to red, of which color and blue it is composed, in equal proportions as to power. In this state of intensity it forms the proper contrasting or neutralizing color to pure yellow. The two primaries of which it is compounded are its melodizing colors. Although red be one of its component parts, it is not a positively warm color, and is very retiring in effect: being also the darkest of the secondary colors, it bears the nearest relation to black or shade, as its contrasting color, yellow, does to white or light. From these qualities, purple is a pleasing color to the eye, in which respect it is second only to green. In its combination with green it produces that soft and useful tertiary color called olive, or blue-hue, and with orange the most powerful of this class, russet, or red-hue.

Purple has, like the other compound colors, various tones, but these are bounded in its approach towards red by crimson, and towards blue by indigo. Its tints have also popular names peculiar to themselves, such as lilac, peach-blossom, and several others.

Purple is not much used as a leading color in decoration, which, I believe, arises from its bad effect in artificial light. It has been already noticed, that all artificial lights, used for economic purposes, are less or more of a warm and yellow tone, as any one may observe in viewing the flame of a candle or gas-lamp in daylight. Yellow being the natural contrast to purple, and being thus diffused over it, neutralizes and injures its effect. Indeed, all cool colors are less or more injured by the effect of such lights, while warm colors, from their being allied to red, are improved in brilliancy. The diagram facing the title, by being viewed in clear daylight, and immediately after in candlelight, will illustrate this fact in a sufficiently satisfactory manner. This effect of artificial light is worthy of particular attention, for it is not only the positive color upon which it is produced, but upon compound hues of every description, according to the predominance of one or other of the primaries in their composition.

Purple may be used in large quantities in any general arrangement, especially when of a cool tone. In the richest patterns of carpets, shawls, and such like pieces of manufacture, its deepest hues are invaluable. Its powers of contrast to all the warm tones of yellow gives them additional warmth and brilliancy, while its natural clearness prevents it from ever appearing dusky or heavy, except under the influence of artificial light.

BLUE is the third of the primary colors, and fifth of the chromatic series. It is, of the primaries, the nearest in relation to shade, as yellow is to light. It is the only absolutely cool color, and communicates this quality to all hues into the combination of which it enters. The contrasting color to blue is the secondary orange, and its melodizing colors in series, green and purple; with the former of which, however, it is more discordant than either of the other two primaries are with either of their melodizing colors. This gives rise to the necessity of a seventh color of a neutral description, which ought generally to be interposed between these two colors when in their perfect state of intensity. This neutral hue is gray, the medium between warmth and coolness, and between light and shade, or black and white.

The tertiary color olive, or blue-hue, from being the medial hue between purple and green, and arising from their combination, has a predominance of blue in its composition, and is, therefore, the tertiary that first occurs in the progress of blue to black, or to negation in shade.

Olive, or blue-hue, individually considered, is soft and unassuming, and is of great use in all arrangements whether of a cool or warm tone. Its effect as a melodizing hue with blue, green, and purple, will be seen by reference to the diagram. But it is in its contrasting powers in the lower hues of warm-toned or brilliant compositions that it is most valuable. It relieves and harmonizes, according to its various tones, the tertiaries—russet, citron, marone, and brown Owing, however, to the discord already noticed, it ought never to be brought into immediate contact with blue, but should be melodized by the introduction of a semi-tonic hue between them. This hue may be a gray of a warm purplish tone, which will melodize best in being blended with the blue, and produce harmony in coming distinctly against the olive in its full warmth. Slate-color is the next hue in the progress of blue down to black, which, from its peculiar nature, cannot be used in any but cool-toned arrangements.

Blue is individually a pleasing and, at the same time, a brilliant color. It may, therefore, be used in any general arrangement of colors, as it is in the coloring of nature, in a much larger proportion than either of the other two primaries. As a leading color in decoration, it is extremely beautiful when in its proper place. For instance, in the drawing-room of a summer residence, especially when lighted from the south, its effect, as a key, is cool and refreshing, as also in bed-rooms of the same description. In all variously-colored manufactures of silk, pure blue, when properly introduced, is both sparkling and pleasing; but in worsted manufactures, its shades and tints are the most useful; but probably from some difficulty in procuring a proper dye, it is seldom, if ever, produced in perfect purity in such fabrics. Pale tints of blue, or any other cool color, ought never to be introduced into warm arrangements. In such cases it ought always to be used in its deepest hues and shades. This ought to be particularly attended to by designers of patterns for manufactures: for the indiscriminate introduction of light cool tints is a prevailing error amongst them. It has already been explained, that warm colors are naturally allied to light, and cool colors to shade Light tints are, therefore, when employed in such designs, enhanced and strengthened by being of a warm tone, and are consequently neutralized and sunk as they approach to that which is cool. In the works of the most eminent artists, this coolness and subordination of the shades, and glowing warmth in the lights, must be apparent to all who have paid any attention to the subject.

GREEN, although the last in the general series which I have adopted, is the medial or second of the secondary colors, because it is a compound of yellow and blue, in equal proportions—the one primary being most allied to light, and the other to shade. Its melodizing colors are of course these two primaries, and its contrasting color the remaining primary, red. As red is the most decided or pre-eminent of the primaries, so green is the most cool and soft of the secondaries, and the most pleasing and agreeable of all decided colors. It is also unlike the other two secondaries in this respect—that, in its approximation to either of its component parts, it produces no other distinct denomination of color—all its tones retaining the same name. Out of the union of green with orange arises the lightest of the tertiary colors, citron; and out of that with purple the deepest, olive, to which it appears particularly allied.

Green is nature's favorite color, prevailing over the face of the landscape to a far greater extent than any other. By a beneficent exercise of the divine wisdom, it is exhibited in its greatest intensity and depth when the sun's rays are most powerful, thereby counteracting the intensity of their reflection, and refreshing the eye by its soft and soothing influence. Green, however, like every other element in nature's coloring, seldom appears in vegetation in its primitive purity—hence the beautiful accordance between the green of the landscape and the blue of the sky, so evidently assisted in both harmony and melody by the intervention of the warm and neutral gray, which prevails intermediately in the distance of the one and the horizon of the other. Green in its various tones, as may naturally be supposed, is a favorite color in decoration, and would be much more so, were it not that in artificial light its effect is much deteriorated, becoming in most cases dull and heavy.

The cause of this I have already explained in treating of yellow and purple. This, however, may in a great measure be avoided by toning it, by keeping it in its proper place, and by selecting proper colors as an accompaniment to it. A rich tone of green upon the walls of a drawing-room, accompanied by cream-color, French-white, and gilding on the cornice, ceiling, and wood-work, with damask hangings of giraffe and gold color, and a suitable carpet, never fails to produce a pleasing and splendid effect in any light. When this arrangement is inverted, that is, when the hangings and chair-seats are green, and the walls of a warm tone, the effect is equally beautiful in daylight; but in artificial light it is injured by the green being neutralized, and the warm tone on the wall rendered more effective; thus making that which is principal in the arrangement, and of the smallest quantity, recede, while that which ought to retire and be subordinate is brought forward. This applies to all other colors employed in decoration, according to their relative powers of reflecting or absorbing such kinds of light.

Of all decided colors, green may be used with most freedom in manufactures. In carpets, especially, it ought almost always to preponderate. They receive the rays of light more directly during the day than any other part of the furniture or decoration; and green in its various hues, is not only in that light most pleasing, but also relieves and harmonizes others more effectually than any other color. Its bright and vivid tones and tints are easily neutralized, and seldom produce crudity or harshness of effect in any arrangement. Rich and deep tones of green, especially when tempered towards a tertiary hue, harmonize with and give value to all descriptions of warm colors. Its cooler hues and shades ought, however, to be used with more caution; for they are apt to appear heavy, and although blue predominates in them to the same extent that it does in the hues of purple called indigo, yet they have not the same clearness.

As already observed, there cannot be produced any other absolutely distinct description of color but one, and that is by a combination of the three primaries, or, what is the same thing, any two of the secondaries. Of the infinite multitude of hues which arise out of the triple combination, I have in another part adopted, as the seventh color, the most neutral of them all, gray. Those tertiary hues that are distinguished by a predominance of one of the primary or secondary colors in their composition, I have noticed in treating of the colors themselves In decorative arrangements, oak may be reckoned of a citron, and mahogany of a russet hue, and they will, of course, bear the relation of these tertiaries to the other colors with which they are associated.

BLACK, as already noticed, is produced by the total interruption of the action which produces light, and its natural contrast is white—being the most perfect state of that action. Black can only be used in large quantities in arrangements of a cool and sombre character, and ought always to be pure and transparent. For want of this quality in the black employed in the generality of worsted fabrics, it has always a sooty and heavy effect. It ought, therefore, to be employed in such manufactures with great caution. Perhaps the most general error in the coloring of the carpets manufactured in this country was, till of late, the too frequent use of black and white. The deepest shades should never go below indigo, marone, or brown, and the highest tints, as already observed, would be much improved by being mellowed down by some warm color. More latitude may be taken with black in the coloring of silk manufactures, as it can be produced on that material in the greatest clearness and depth. Its use in modern decoration is rather limited, being generally confined to chair-seats, door-mountings, and dining-room chimney-pieces.

In the decorative painting, however, of Pompeii and Herculaneum, it was used in large quantities; and in combination with the intense and brilliant colors which accompanied it, produced the most splendid effect. This evidently resulted from the perfect knowledge possessed by the decorators of that period of the relative powers of their materials, which seem to have been in their hands what the keys of a powerful organ would at the present period be in those of an accomplished musician. Yet this use of the brightest and deepest colors, by the ancient Roman, was perhaps more a particular characteristic of style, than a beauty in their decorative coloring. But, as already observed, it was the best adapted to their clear skies, and, in some cases, uncovered apartments.

Black, and its contrasting hue, white, are the two most dangerous elements in the whole chromatic series; the one being at the bottom and the other at the top of the scale; and particular care is, therefore, required in their management.

When an arrangement of rich and intense colors is here and there interrupted by patches or shadings of black, as too often happens in patterns of carpets and other subjects of a similar nature, the effect is harsh and unpleasant. It ought, therefore, in all such designs, to be accompanied and mellowed by those deep hues that lie next in the natural series. White should in like manner, as before noticed, be introduced by a gradation of the lightest tints, otherwise the effect will be spotty and broken.

It is very difficult to give rules that will be applicable in all cases, but it is trusted the above will be of some use in the general practice of the decorator and manufacturer.

PART II.

ON THE PRACTICE OF HOUSE-PAINTING.

THE principles which operate in the production of beauty in the art of house-painting, constitute a branch of the science of Æsthetics, with which the public are becoming daily more acquainted; but the practical department of this art is still enveloped in mystery. Such mystery, however, ought not to exist in a country like Great Britain, where this department of house-painting cannot fail to be a subject of general interest, inasmuch as it is calculated to enhance greatly the durability of our dwelling-houses and public buildings, and the comfort of their occupants, by preserving them from the effects of a changeable climate and humid atmosphere.

In this country the ceilings and walls of the apartments in our dwelling-houses and other buildings are almost uniformly finished in plaster. Now, it is well known that this composition is remarkable for its great facility in absorbing moisture. Consequently, when an unpainted plastered apartment is left for any length of time without the benefit of a fire, or heated air supplied by other means, a portion of that humidity with which our atmosphere is generally loaded will be absorbed, and the room thereby rendered unwholesome, and its wood-fittings, as well as the plaster itself, impaired in durability.

The first and most important object in decorating a house is, therefore, to render its interior walls impervious to this absorption, and the most effectual way to do this is to paint them. Important as this operation is, it is often mismanaged to such an extent that families are put to all the inconvenience, trouble, and expense of a thorough painting several times during the best part of a lifetime, where once might suffice. The cause of this shall now be shown.

The materials employed by the house-painter, in what is termed plain painting, are—

WHITE-LEAD,	LAKE,
LITHARGE,	CALCOTHAR OR VITRIOL,
SUGAR-OF-LEAD,	VENETIAN RED,
RED-LEAD,	SPANISH BROWN,
ORANGE-LEAD,	PRUSSIAN BLUE,
CHROME-YELLOW,	FRENCH ULTRAMARINE,
CHROME-GREEN,	TURKEY UMBER,
YELLOW-OCHRE,	ENGLISH UMBER,
TERRA-DI-SIENA,	LAMP-BLACK,
INDIAN RED,	LINSEED OIL,
VERMILION,	SPIRITS OF TURPENTINE.

With the nature, properties, and varieties of each of these ingredients used in the compounding of paint I shall endeavor to make the reader acquainted.

WHITE-LEAD forms, or ought to form, the body of almost all light-colored paints, often constituting nine-tenths of the composition. It is a carbonate of the metal from which it takes its name, and is prepared by exposing thin plates of cast lead to the action of the vapor of ascetic acid, air, and carbonic acid. Other processes are employed for the same purpose, but it is by this process only that the resulting carbonate of lead is obtained of that degree of density and opacity, and that perfect freedom from crystalline texture, which properly fit it for paint. This is called the Dutch process, and was introduced into England about the year 1780. It is fully described, together with the other processes, in Brande's *Manual of Chemistry*, fifth edition, p. 844. The quality of this article ought to be considered of the greatest importance by the house-painter, as upon it depends the durability of his work; yet it is, of all the materials he employs, the most difficult to be obtained in an unadulterated state. For all general purposes he procures it ground in oil to the consistency of a thick paste, which is produced by mixing the carbonate in a damp state with refined linseed oil, and passing them through a mill, in which they are properly amalgamated. It is in this process that adulteration takes place. Formerly fine chalk or whiting used to be employed by the manufacturer to cheapen this article, but when thus adulterated, the presence of the chalk was detected by its specific gravity. While this mode was in use, the late Sir John Robison, secretary to the Royal Society of Edinburgh, being elected a commissioner of police, had a small vessel filled with genuine white-lead and a similar vessel filled with that which was procured by contract for the city works, and the difference of gravity was found to be several ounces in the pound-weight. But the possibility of detecting the adulteration of white-lead is now rendered very difficult, from its being reduced by the admixture of a cheap mineral substance called sulphate of baryta, which resembles lead in its gravity, but not in its density and opacity, and is now very largely employed in this way. Therefore the painter, who by competition must work at low rates, is naturally liable to be tempted by the offer of white-lead below the market price, by which he effects a small saving in his material, while the employer sustains a great loss from the want of proper durability in the work. The only mode of detecting the presence of baryta in white-lead is by its insolubility in dilute nitric acid, pure lead being entirely dissolved by it. But this is rather a difficult process when the paint is in its manufactured state, and the only way in which a painter can be quite safe is to make his orders worthy of the manufacturer's particular attention, by giving the highest price, as also by taking a large quantity at a time, in which case it may be warranted free of adulteration.

For the thick paste into which white-lead is ground by the manufacturer, the painter reduces it, by means of linseed oil and spirits of turpentine, to that consistency more properly called paint, as shall afterwards be explained.

Lead supplies to the painter other materials besides its carbonate.

LITHARGE, the fused oxide of that metal, made by the simple action of heat and air in the process of extracting silver from lead, is used as a drying ingredient in the first coats of paint employed upon wood and plaster; and when linseed oil is boiled for coarse out-door work, litharge is dissolved in it for the same purpose

SUGAR-OF-LEAD, another dryer, is made by exposing lead to the fumes of vinegar or pyroligneous acid—dissolving the white powder thus produced in excess of acid, and then crystallizing it.

RED-LEAD and ORANGE-LEAD are other oxides

of lead produced from litharge, and are converted into paint by being mixed with linseed oil, and reduced to a smooth paste by the painter. This he performs by spreading the red-lead, when mixed with the oil, upon a slab of Arbroath pavement-stone, of about thirty inches square, and working it over this surface by means of another stone, called a muller, which is of a conical form, with a base of about five inches diameter; it is generally made of whinstone, and held between the hands of the painter while triturating the paint between it and the slab. Litharge and sugar-of-lead are also submitted to the same process before being mixed with the paint. Lead unites with iron, with the alkalies, and with earth, in producing the chrome colors, which are—

CHROME-YELLOW of various tones, from the clearest lemon to the deepest orange color. This pigment is made by adding a limpid solution of the chromate of potash to a solution, equally limpid, of acetate, or nitrate of lead; and the tones of its color are deepened by the addition of subacetate of lead, or rendered pale by a solution of alum or sulphuric acid, in the course of their manufacture. There are also reds, blues, and greens, which are chromates, and made by processes of a somewhat similar nature, but the yellow is by far the most important to the house-painter—being almost the only bright yellow now in use. Like most other manufactured colors, it varies greatly both in quality and price; and the only security the painter can have for its being genuine, and of the finest quality, is to purchase it from a manufacturer of high respectability, and give the highest price. It comes from the manufacturer in dry lumps, and is converted into paint by the process already described.

The OCHRES are another class of yellows of which there is great variety. They are a native earthy mixture of silica and alumina, colored by oxide of iron, with occasionally a little calcareous matter and magnesia, and are found between strata of rock and sand. Ochre varies in color from a light tint of tempered yellow to a tempered red, and in price from 1d. to 1s. per lb.

Yellow-ochre may be made of a dull red-hue by being gently calcined. Native red-ochre is called red chalk, but is never converted into a pigment. The lower qualities of ochre are found in large quantities in this country, and are used for mixing the commonest kinds of paints for out-door work, floor-cloths, &c. The finest quality is found at Siena, in Italy, and is called—

TERRA-DI-SIENA. This species of ochre is as useful to the professor of high art as it is to the house-painter. It has great density, without opacity, and produces delicate tints when mixed with white paint, or when used as a transparent color upon a light groundwork. The house-painter who wishes to do ample justice to his employer, should use no other yellows for interior painting besides chrome-yellow of the best kind, and *terra di Siena*, because by these two pigments every color or hue, of which yellow is an element, may be produced, and because they are the only yellows that can be depended upon for durability.

When calcined, *terra di Siena* forms one of the most beautiful hues of reddish-orange or brown, which is as useful in producing tints, by its admixture with white paint, as it is by its transparency in giving richness to shades when used as a glazing color.

Of Reds there are many kinds, principally

manufactured. Perhaps the only native red, besides the burnt ochres, converted into a pigment by the house-painter, is Indian Red.

INDIAN RED is brought to England in its native state, which is that of a very rich iron ore, full of gritty particles, but of these it is generally freed before being converted into paint. It is of various tones, but all of a slightly purplish character, and when reduced, by being mixed with white paint, produces very delicate tints. It is not transparent, and, consequently, cannot be reduced to a tint in any other way. It is, like most other native colors, remarkable for its permanency; and it, as well as the other native colors, are converted into paint by the same process explained in reference to the manufactured colors.

Cinnabar is the native red sulphuret of mercury, but is superseded in its use as a pigment by the factitious cinnabar, called Vermilion, which, like the native kind, is a compound of mercury and sulphur.

VERMILION is manufactured in England, Holland, and other parts of Europe, but the finest quality is manufactured in China, which, however, is often adulterated before it reaches the hands of the painter. Field says of this color: "It is true that vermilions have obtained the double disrepute of fading in a strong light, and of becoming black or dark by time or impure air; but colors, like characters, suffer contamination and disrepute from bad association; it has happened, accordingly, that vermilion which has been rendered lakey or crimson by mixture with lake or carmine, has faded in the light, and that when it has been toned to the scarlet hue by red or orange lead, it has afterwards become blackened in impure air, &c. Hence the ill fame of vermilion both with authors and artists."*

Real Chinese vermilion is a permanent and a beautiful color—it is an impalpable powder, possessing great density and opacity when mixed as a paint, but from the ease with which it is adulterated, and the consequent difficulty of obtaining it pure in this country, it is requisite to commission it direct from China in order to insure its being genuine: it costs in China about 4s. 10d. per pound. Its price in this country

* Field's Chromatography, &c., see p. 93.

varies from three shillings to six shillings per pound.

LAKE is another manufactured red used by the house painter. Its tones vary from scarlet to crimson, and the methods by which it is produced are very numerous. The best lake is made from cochineal, and the worst is made by the precipitation of tinctures of Brazil-wood and other dyeing drugs, upon alumina and other earths. The best lake is made in China, but it can be so well imitated, in all but its durability, by the European manufacturer, that it is very difficult to be had, being seldom brought down to any of the Chinese ports with which we trade.*

Lake is transparent, and more used in that way, than mixed as a tint with white-lead. When used as a crimson for polychrome work upon ceilings, it is mixed with spirits of turpentine instead of oil, because the spirits hold a greater body of it in solution; but this shall be explained more fully in the sequel. Lake varies in price accord-

* As a proof of this, I may mention, that within the last three years, I have sent orders both to Canton and Hong Kong for lake, which have not yet been executed, while there was no difficulty in regard to vermilion.

ing to quality, from ten shillings to sixty shillings the pound-weight. Some of the beautiful madder lakes made by Field are, I believe, much more expensive, but they are only for the palette of the professor of high art.

Rose-pink is a coarse kind of lake, produced by dyeing chalk or whiting with decoction of Brazil-wood, but it is only fit for paper-staining.

Colcothar of Vitriol, the purplish red peroxide of iron, made by adding solution of soda to the solution of sulphate of iron or copperas, is another red used by the house-painter. It produces the chocolate paint so much in use for the wood-work of kitchens, servants' halls, &c. It is cheap in price, and very durable. This substance, when carefully washed, is the rouge of the silversmith.

Venetian Red, Light-Red, and Spanish Brown, are burnt ochres of coarse quality, and used by the house-painter as red pigments.

A native Blue is unknown in the art of house-painting. Indeed, there are only two native pigments of this color, namely, Saunder's blue, found near copper-mines, which has the defect of turning green when mixed with oil, and blue-ochre, a subphosphate of iron found in Cornwall and in North America. Field says: "What Indian red is to the color red, and Oxford ochre to yellow, this color is to the color blue." But it is not in general use, or easily procurable.

PRUSSIAN BLUE is one of the most important pigments to the house-painter as a manufactured blue. It is the percyanide of iron, and is produced by heating to redness dried blood, or other animal matter, with an equal weight of pearl ash, till reduced to a paste, which is again reduced with water, filtered, and mixed with a solution of one part of proto-sulphate of iron and two parts of alum. The precipitate of this is greenish, but it absorbs oxygen from the atmosphere which completes the process. It is a deep and powerful color, mixing well with white paint in the production of all tints of which blue is an element, and is at the same time decidedly transparent. It is, like most other manufactured pigments, of various qualities.

FACTITIOUS ULTRAMARINE is now much used by the higher class of house-painters, where richness, brilliancy, and permancy of color are required. There are various qualities of this pigment, and it is consequently sold at various prices, from five shillings to forty shillings a pound; but that made by Guimet, who invented it in 1828, is decidedly the best, and is never, when genuine, sold below the highest price. This is very little inferior to the lazulite (*lapis lazuli*) ultramarine, used in high art. It was made by Guimet in the following manner: A mixture of sulphur and dry carbonate of soda was heated to redness; when the mass fused, another mixture of silicate of soda and aluminate of soda was sprinkled into it by degrees. The crucible in which this was performed was then again exposed for an hour to the fire, by which time the ultramarine was formed, only it contained a little sulphur, which was separated by means of water. Various other processes have since been invented, all proving that ultramarine is a compound of silicate of alumina, silicate of soda, and sulphurate of sodium, the color being the result of the reaction of the latter constituent upon the two former. The blue of the diagram is Guimet's ultramarine.

One of the most useful pigments in the hands of the house-painter is Umber, of which there are two kinds—Turkey umber and English umber.

TURKEY UMBER is decidedly the best of the two. It is a variety of ochraceous iron ore, chiefly brought from Cypress, and is of a grayish tone of brown, approaching yellow-hue. It is of great density, producing a variety of beautifully chaste tints when mixed with white paint, and assisting the drying of all paints of which it forms a constituent. When calcined, its color approaches more the tone of russet or red-hue, and is, in its burnt state as well as in its native state, the most efficient pigment in the production of all varieties of drab and stone color. The inferior umber called English, is a native earth found in Derbyshire, Somersetshire, and other parts of England, and is used instead of Turkey umber upon low-priced work.

The *media* or vehicles by which these pigments are mixed, when applied in house-painting, are first, linseed oil; secondly, a mixture of linseed-oil with spirits of turpentine; and, thirdly, spirits of turpentine alone, with some drying ingredient.

These drying ingredients are litharge and sugar-of-lead, already noticed, and a kind of varnish called japanner's gold-size, made of the refuse of gum copal, or gum animà, litharge, and umber dissolved by heat in linseed-oil and spirits of turpentine, thoroughly amalgamated and purified.

LINSEED-OIL is the only oil used by the house-painter. It is, as its name implies, produced from linseed. The following is the process: The seed is first bruised, either by the original mode of being pounded in hard wooden mortars by pestles shod with iron, set in motion by carns, driven by horse or water power, or by hydraulic mill. The seed thus triturated, is put into woollen bags, which are again wrapped up in hair-cloths, and the oil expressed, either by these bags being squeezed between upright wedges in press-boxes, by the impulsion of vertical rams driven by the same mechanism, or subjected to the more powerful operation of the hydraulic press.

This material varies little in quality, and is not

liable to be adulterated. The only superiority of one kind over another is in its age and clearness; for where a large stock is kept, it is found that in about six months there is a considerable accumulation of refuse at the bottom of the cistern, which is only fit to be employed in mixing coarse paint for out-door work. Linseed-oil varies greatly in price, according to the demand for the cake which is necessarily manufactured along with it, and is used for fattening cattle, as also according to the state of the seed market, sometimes changing from £25 to £40 per tun, in the course of a few months; so that the tradesman whose capital and premises enable him to take the advantage of the market, often effects a great saving upon this article.

Linseed-oil is sometimes boiled with litharge to make it dry quick, but when it is thus treated, it is unfit for good work, as shall afterwards be shown.

Spirits of Turpentine is now much used as a vehicle by the house-painter. This oleaginous spirit is extracted from the semi-liquid resinous substance which exudes from a certain species of *pinus*, or fir tree. It is separated from the resin, by being distilled along with water, and is color-less, limpid, and very volatile, having a peculiar, but not disagreeable nor unwholesome smell. Its quality depends upon its freedom from holding any of the resin in solution, with which it was combined while in its native state. The price of spirits of turpentine is as fluctuating as that of linseed-oil.

These are the materials used by the house-painter in the manufacture of that covering intended to secure the plaster and wood finishings of buildings from the injurious effects of a changeable climate and a humid atmosphere. The methods by which they are applied to this purpose shall next be explained.

ON THE METHODS OF EXECUTING PLAIN PAINTING.

THE mixing and laying on of the materials just treated of may with as much propriety be looked upon in the light of a manufacture, as the making of paper or the spinning and weaving of cotton, flax, or wool into cloth; because the painter produces a fabric which will be either coarse or fine, durable or otherwise, according to the quality of the materials mixed together in the paint, and the manner in which they are manipulated in their application, as is the case with other manufactured fabrics.

A painter can easily mix two pots of paint, of which no builder, superintendent of building, nor even a painter himself, unless of much experience, could, in looking upon them, form an opinion as to their comparative value; yet they would bear the same relative value to each other that two equal quantities of paper-maker's pulp would bear, one of which was intended for making the best drawing-paper, and the other for the commonest printing or writing paper—perhaps their relative value might be as one to two. Now, the paint in the one pot, that was not above half the value of that in the other, would, from its want of density and body, spread over a much larger surface of wood or plaster work, than the more expensive mixture just as the inferior pulp would make by får the greatest surface of paper. The product of the paper-maker can be examined in the hand, looked through, and tested in various ways as to the quality of the material employed, whilst the quantity in a given superficies is ascertained by the pound-weight of substance. But this is not the case with the product of the painter; the various coats agreed to be put upon the wood and plaster of a building cannot be taken off and looked through nor examined in any way to find out their quality, neither can the quantity of material in a given surface be guessed at, so that he may receive the same price per yard for the greater number produced by the pot of low-priced paint that he would receive for the smaller number produced by the high-priced pot of paint, or may reduce his rates in proportion to the saving effected in material and workmanship. This is one cause of such differences being found in the estimates of painters when brought into competition for work. The most unscrupulous have always the best chance where no other distinction except that of price is made. The following is the proper mode of proceeding in the manufacture of this fabric upon plaster work, the description of which will equally apply to the painting of wood-work, only the latter is less absorbent.

White-lead ground into a thick paste, as already described, is reduced, by mixing it with linseed-oil, to the consistency of thin cream, adding as a dryer a little litharge ground in oil, as described, and sometimes a little red-lead. This is called the priming, or first coat of paint. If on applying this the plaster be found very absorbent, so that in passing the brush over it in spreading out the priming, the oil is so quickly absorbed as to leave the white-lead rough and dry upon the surface, more oil should be added to the mixture in order that the plaster may be deeply saturated. To prevent this absorption, some painters use boiled oil in their priming, but this is not doing the work justice, for when the oil is boiled it is more viscid, and does not penetrate so far into the plaster, but runs smoothly over the surface. Raw oil, being limpid, penetrates the plaster less or more according to the facility with which it is absorbed, and, when dry, thus far hardens the wall; but boiled oil, being more unctuous and viscid, forms only a thin film, or, if it penetrates at all, it is but a short way. It is sometimes found requisite, when the plaster has a very close skin upon it, to mix a little spirits of turpentine with the priming, to help the absorption; but such cases are of rare occurrence.

There is a practice amongst painters which, in some cities, where the prices of their work is much reduced, prevails to a great extent. It is this. They wash over the plaster and woodwork (especially the former) with a weak solution of glue, called size, before the application of the first coat of paint; this prevents the absorption of the oil, and causes the paint to spread over a much greater surface than it would have done had this preparation not been applied. This practice is very injurious to the work (especially the plaster) by depriving it of that hardening which the absorption of the linseed-oil produces. The paint, even supposing it to be good, forms little more than a thin weak film, which is effectually separated from the plaster by the thin pellicle of glue below it; whereas, in the absence of this preparation, the absorption of the oil leaves the paint like a firmly united crust upon the surface of both wood and plaster. (Note B.)

We shall, however, suppose that the priming or first coat of paint has been properly mixed, and applied, and allowed to stand for a few days to harden. The number of days will depend upon the temperature kept up in the apartment, upon the weather, and also upon the absorption that has taken place; the experienced painter only can say when the second coat ought to be applied.

The second coat should be made thicker than the first; but its particular degree of relative thickness will depend upon the degree of absorption that has taken place in the application of the first coat. Sometimes a great proportion of it bears out—that is, dries with a gloss; in which case the second coat ought to have a good body of white lead in it. At other times, it is found that no part of the first coat bears out, and that even some portions of it have had the oil so completely absorbed as to leave nothing on the surface but a dry powder. When this is the case, it is a sure sign that the plaster is of such a nature as to receive the full benefit of the oil; and, that it may be properly saturated, the paint for the second coat is kept rather thin. Before applying this coat, the work should be rubbed with fine sand-paper. If the second coat bears out properly when dry, the third coat will form the groundwork for the finishing process; but should it not bear out properly, the work will be understood to require five coats; and, therefore, another coat of plain oil-paint is applied.

The groundwork for finishing upon is composed of white-lead, diluted with equal parts of linseed-oil and spirits of turpentine; the thinness of the latter enabling a greater body of white-lead to be held in solution, and thus increasing the density of the mixture. Into this such ground pigments are put as will alter the white paint to a tint of the color in which the work is to be finished, along with a little sugar-of-lead as a dryer. This tint is made deeper than the intended finishing-coat, by which means the solidity and durability of the color is increased. The thicker this coat is made, and the more it is spread out with the brush, the more durable will be the fabric, and the finer will be its surface.

In some establishments, the workmen are allowed to bestow more time and labor on twenty square yards of surface, than they are in others allowed to bestow on double that quantity.

This ground color is generally dry enough to receive the finishing-coat on the second day after it is applied, and should not stand above a few days, as its becoming too dry prevents that incorporation of these two coats, so essential to equality in the opacity or deadness of the surface and to the solidity of the tint.

The finishing-coat is white-lead in the state of a thick paste, already described, diluted with spirits of turpentine only, and mixed with such ground pigments as produce the desired tint, to which is added a little sugar-of-lead or japan gold-size as a dryer. This species of paint, when of a light tint, is of great density, and as, from the volatility of the spirits of turpentine, it soon thickens after leaving the brush, great precision and despatch must be employed in applying it. This is the only coat of paint that, in finished work, meets the eye of the spectator, and he cannot, from looking at it, have any idea of those that are underneath, and upon which the durability of the work principally depends. This underwork may be worth fourpence a yard, or it may be worth ninepence a yard, and the surface of the finishing-coat look equally well. This, as well as the variety in the quality of pigments, sufficiently accounts for the variable durability of paint work—some houses requiring to be re-painted in four or five years, while others will require little more than washing for twenty-five or even thirty years.

This method of finishing is called flatted painting, and is now sometimes stippled, by being wrought over with the point of a dry brush immediately after being laid upon the work in the usual way, which gives it an equal and fine surface. In almost all that kind of painting improperly called *cheap painting*, as also in all cases where a painter agrees to finish new work with three coats of paint—a coat of size is introduced between the first and second, or between the second and third coats. This is not so destructive of the quality of the work as the application of size before the first coat, but it is bad enough, and is a practice that ought on no account to be resorted to. It is this practice that so often, in the re-painting of a house, causes the necessity of removing the old paint entirely; because, if this be not done, the coats of the old paint separate where these sizings have taken place, and come chipping off along with the new painting which has been put above them. Thus a heavy extra expense is incurred where a considerable saving ought to have been effected; for good old painting, when properly polished down, forms the best groundwork for new painting.

Where there are knots in wood-work, it is requisite, before priming it, to secure the resin which is concentrated in them. This is now done by means of covering them with a species of varnish made by dissolving gum-lac in spirits of wine; and, as a further security against the resin coming through the paint, leaf metal is fixed above this varnish by means of japan gold-size.

ON THE MATERIALS EMPLOYED IN ORNAMENTAL PAINTING.

Having endeavored to make the reader in some degree acquainted with the varieties of materials employed by the house-painter, and the various modes in which he applies them in what is termed plain painting, I shall now give some account of the ornamental department, in which is included the imitating of woods and marbles. But before entering upon this part of my subject it is requisite to state, that besides the pigments already enumerated, other two are required in imitating woods. These are Vandyke-brown and ivory-black. The first of these is a species of bog earth of a fine deep tone, and semi-transparent; and the second an animal charcoal, produced by burning ivory in close vessels—a pigment as valuable to the professor of high art as to the humble imitator of nature's more minute beauty in the grains of wood.

COPAL VARNISH is also a most important material connected with this department of the art of house-painting, and also sometimes added to plain painting, by which the beauty and durability of such work is greatly enhanced. There is no material in which the painter has greater latitude as to quality and price than this; and certainly none in which the inexperienced are more likely to be deceived, or the selection of which requires more care on the part of the most experienced.

The best copal varnish is made by dissolving the finest gum-copal in clarified linseed oil and spirits of turpentine. The process by which the amalgamation of these ingredients takes place is both difficult and uncertain in its operation. When this varnish is made so as to dry quickly, gum animà and sugar-of-lead are added to the ingredients already named.

Gum copal is the produce of three or four different kinds of trees, and is therefore, in itself, of different qualities. But all its varieties being very expensive, many other ingredients are introduced into this varnish by the manufacturer, in order to cheapen it. The various qualities thus produced are sold to the painter at prices varying from eight shillings to twenty-four shillings a gallon. This is the latitude afforded by the manufacturer, but it is well known that the painter can reduce the cheapest quality to a still lower degree, by the introduction of boiled linseed oil, a practice the bad effects of which become apparent in about a year after the work is finished.

No painter can judge of the quality of copal varnish by merely examining it. Indeed, so uncertain is the operation of making it, that the manufacturer himself must submit it to various practical tests before he can with safety put it into the hands of those tradesmen whose custom he is anxious to retain. From this cause some of the larger manufacturers have on hand from twenty to thirty different qualities of copal varnish, which they apportion to their various customers according to the price given, the quantity generally ordered, and the certainty of payment; often making the price of an inferior, equal to that of a superior quality, in order to recover the risk of a bad debt.

This varnish, when of the best quality, is a clear limpid fluid, capable of hardening without losing its transparency. It gives a lustre to the work upon which it is spread, and adds greatly to its durability in defending it from the action of the air. Really good varnish becomes quite hard, does not crack, does not become discolored by age, and does not lose its lustre for many years, whilst inferior varnishes either do not harden, crack, or soon lose their lustre, and expose to decay the work upon which they are applied.

A coat of fine copal varnish, applied upon stippled plain painting, not only greatly enhances its effect, by giving it the appearance of enamel, but renders it of a doubly durable nature, without adding greatly to the expense.

OF IMITATIONS OF WOODS AND MARBLES.

MANY people of highly cultivated minds have a dislike to imitations of woods and marbles in house-painting. This must arise from the imperfect manner in which these imitations are often executed—the most monotonous plainness being more endurable to a correct and well-educated eye, than an imperfect imitation of nature.

If certain woods and marbles be beautiful in themselves, and if they be chosen for the fitting up of the interiors of edifices, as much on account of the gratification they afford the eye, as from any other quality they possess, what reasonable objection can be raised to the appropriate substitution of a good imitation, where the reality cannot be had? What are the lath-and-plaster divisions, and the stucco-mouldings and rosettes on the ceilings of a building in any of the classical styles of architecture, but an imitation of the manner in which the ancients constructed their marble soffits? How often do we see, in other styles of architecture, the construction of wood-work imitated in lath and plaster! How often do we find apparently strong beams supported by trusses crossing from wall to wall of an apartment, which beams seem to support others of a lighter kind which cross them above, and form the ceiling into panels, all constructed of lath and plaster! Surely ceilings may be as appropriately painted in imitaton of marble or wood as constructed in imitation of these materials! Indeed, when the material is imitated in the construction, the design of the architect cannot be complete until the painter's imitation follows. (Note C.)

The humble art of imitating woods and marbles is in some measure allied to the high art of portrait-painting, in being also an imitative art, and requiring a degree of natural genius in the grainer, as such artists are technically called, to enable him to avoid the fault so common in both arts, namely, that of producing a caricature of the object of which he attempts to produce a correct resemblance. It is well known that there are a great number of painters of cheap portraits, whose professional practice lies amongst a class of society not remarkable for their appreciation of works of art. The productions of such geniuses are almost sure to stare one in the face on entering the public-room of an hotel or tavern, in the caricatured resemblance of the landlord, accompanied sometimes by his beloved wife, respected mother, or interesting children, all as stiff and flat as if cut out of pasteboard. It requires but a slight knowledge of art to feel that such productions, were they often obtruded on the notice of the well-educated and refined, would, in the course of time, embue their minds with something like a dislike to portrait-painting generally. Fortunately for this art, however, the works of this class of portrait painters are not often necessarily obtruded upon the notice of the higher classes.

It is not so with respect to the artists who imitate that species of nature's endless beauties, which the various kinds of woods and marbles exhibit; the mere mechanic and the man of genius in this branch of art have very generally an equal chance of having their work placed before the highest classes of society, occasionally in their own mansions, but oftener in our churches and public buildings, which being generally painted according to what is erroneously supposed to be the cheapest estimate, are of course in the lowest style of the art.

In the graining department there are artists who excel in woods, and others in marbles; some excel in imitating one kind of wood only, some in one kind of marble, others in two or three, and very rarely one who excels in all the varieties of both. The wages of these artists vary from twenty shillings to forty shillings a week, so that, in sufficiently large establishments, the value of the work may be greatly enhanced by placing the various kinds of imitation in the hands of the best qualified artists. It often happens, however, that the consideration of these, and all other facilities for producing superior work which some establishments may possess, are set aside, and offers asked from five or six painters, whose materials, workmen, and style of execution, differ much more widely than the amounts of their estimates. Thus it often happens, that where great expense has been incurred in the architectural decoration of a building, we find painting of the lowest class, both as to want of durability in the plain painting, and of artistic feeling in the imitation-work and other branches of the ornamental department.

To abolish imitations of woods and marbles in house-painting because they are so often badly done, would be a retrograde movement in this important branch of the useful arts. It would be much better for people of taste to endeavor to improve the practice of this department by taking some interest in it, and becoming sufficiently acquainted with its nature to enable them to judge between the good and the bad, the true, and the false.

The wood or plaster upon which an imitation of wood or marble is to be produced, is, or ought to be, painted in four or five coats, by the process already explained, with this difference, that the last coat is not diluted entirely with spirits of turpentine, but partly with oil, and that in applying it, a still greater degree of care is requisite to avoid leaving any marks of the brush upon its surface. It thus requires much more time to paint work for grounds of this description than for plain finishing.

In imitating oak this groundwork is tinted of such a color as may be suitable to the tone of the oak intended to be imitated; for there is great variety in the wood itself, both as to tone and depth, so that the painter can adopt that which is most suitable to the light, the aspect, and the furnishings of the apartment. The tones of this wood vary from a tint of yellow, yellow-hue, or orange-hue, to deep shades of the two latter, for all those tints and shades are to be found in various specimens of the natural wood. Hence it is, that imitation-oak is one of the best media for a general arrangement of color in an apartment; and the more especially, because this wood may be imitated upon the ceiling, walls, or wood-fittings of any apartment—all these parts being often constructed of real oak.

When the groundwork is quite dry, a thick unctuous mixture of semi-transparent paint is prepared, varying in its tone and depth according to that of the kind of oak to be imitated. This is laid equally and smoothly over the groundwork, after which a toothed instrument made of steel, ivory, horn, or wood (for all these kinds of graining-combs, as they are technically named, are in use), is drawn through this composition, by which it is separated upon the groundwork into minute portions, representing the grain of the wood. As this grain is open or close in the real oak, according to the modes in which the tree has been cut, the graining-combs are made various in the breadth of their teeth.

The larger transverse septa of oak are, in general, very distinct, producing beautiful flowers when cut obliquely, and these are imitated by the painter either by wiping off portions of the grained paint with a cloth, or washing it off with spirits of turpentine. This part of the process requires some taste in the choice of the configuration of the champs, or flowers, as they are called, because in the natural wood they are found in great variety.

In this simple matter it is astonishing to mark the variety that exists in the tastes of the grainers, and how an apprentice boy, from intuitive feeling, will sometimes surpass the most experienced workman in giving beautiful forms to the flowers.

When the grain of the wood is thus completed it is allowed to dry, after which it is lightly shaded with transparent brown, either in oil or water color. This part of the process is technically called glazing, and completes the imitation, which is then varnished with copal varnish. In cheap work the flowering, the glazing, and the varnishing are, one or other, and sometimes all, dispensed with, there being nothing above the plain painting but the graining substance, whilst the ground-work, instead of being four or five coats of good paint, is produced by one coat of glue-size and two coats of inferior paint. Boiled linseed-oil, with a little *dryer* in it, is sometimes used on such work instead of copal varnish.

Imitation mahogany is painted upon grounds varying from a low-toned tint of orange color to a deep hue of yellowish red. The grainer provides himself with *terra-di-Siena*, Turkey umber, Vandyke brown, ivory-black, and lake, each being ground to an impalpable paste in water. One or more of these he mixes with small beer, or any other slightly tenacious liquid, to a thin stain. With this he imitates the natural pores of the wood, by laying it on in small portions, and, while it is wet, stippling it carefully with a dry crush. The stain is then made deeper, and its tone enriched and applied in masses, to represent the beautifully variable shades for which mahogany is so remarkable. These shades he softens, by working upon them slightly with a brush made of badgers' hair, called a softener, which operation must be performed with despatch, as the process must be completed upon each divisible portion of the work while the stain is in a fluid state. The shading is often greatly enhanced by being produced with two tones of staining-color simultaneously—the one light and cool, and the other deep and warm, but to perform this propely, requires great taste and dexterity on the part of the artist.

Immediately after this shading is dry, the reeded grain of the wood is given by a light cool-toned stain, in a thin flat brush being lightly drawn over the shades and gently softened with the badger-hair brush. Should the shades be deep, the whole is then secured by a coat of some thin binding substance that will sufficiently penetrate the water-color and bind it to the ground-work, but if light, the varnish itself will be sufficient. This ought to be of the finest quality of copal varnish.

Satin-wood is imitated by a similar process to that employed in imitating mahogany, with the exception of that part which produces the effect of pores. The ground-work for satin-wood is a light tint of yellow.

Maple-wood is imitated in the same way. The

effect of the small bird-eye knots, and apparent light and shade by which they are accompanied, being produced by the points and sides of the artist's fingers while the stain is in a fluid state. The ground is a very light tint of yellowish pink or cream-color.

Some artists introduce the shades and veins of the heart of the tree, especially in imitating Spanish mahogany and maple-wood, but this requires to be done with great taste and judgment, otherwise, plain shades and veins are much to be preferred.

Imitation rose-wood is not so often introduced in house-painting as it used to be. It is done upon a ground-work of a deep hue of yellowish red, and the stain is made of ivory-black, and applied with thin flat graining-brushes, like the over-grain of mahogany, and sometimes with sable-hair pencils set in a case. It is afterwards shaded, secured, and finished with the finest copal varnish.

Imitation oak has been greatly used in halls, staircases, libraries, and dining-rooms, and it will be observed, from the description of the process, that it must be very durable, especially that part of it by which the pores or grain of the wood is represented. The varnish used upon it is not necessarily of the finest quality, but ought still to be unadulterated copal varnish. When, however, it is desired to have a superior lustre, or to be polished in the style of a coach panel, which it is sometimes, the finest quality only should be used.

Imitation mahogany, from its greater beauty, and from the growing taste for full-toned coloring, is now often employed, instead of oak, as a decorative painting for the wood-work of such apartments as I have just enumerated. Mahogany, like oak, is to be found of various tints, shades, and tones of its particular hue. Its imitation may, therefore, be adapted to almost any style of furnishing.

Imitations of maple-wood and satin-wood are used almost exclusively on the wood-work of drawing-rooms and boudoirs, and although they cannot be varied in tone to the extent of either oak or mahogany, yet there is a sufficient latitude to enable the decorator to render either of them harmonious with the peculiar tones of the colors with which they are to be associated. The finest copal varnish should always be used upon imitations of all the fine kinds of woods, by which their durability and beauty will be greatly enhanced.

To imitate marble well, requires, on the part of the artist, an intuitive feeling for beauty in both form and color. The veins of some marbles often exhibit great beauty in their ramifications, and often produce very beautiful forms by their intersecting each other: such as the white-veined, the Siena, the black and gold, and some others. Marbles of the breccia kind, such as the *verd-antique*, the *rosso-antico*, and almost all other conglomerates of the same description, are masses of various indefinite forms, and the success of the artist depends greatly upon the character he gives these forms, and the skill with which he at the same time imparts to the mass that distinguishing feature in all nature's works—infinite variety.

The imitating of marbles enables the house-painter to break his colors, and thus impart to them a quality, the value of which is well known to professors of the higher branches of the art of painting. The colors of marbles are various, and amongst them are to be found representatives of the six positive colors, in various degrees of intensity of hue, of tint, and of shade. For instance, we have yellow and orange in some of their most beautiful varieties in *giallo-antico*, or *Siena*; varieties of red in *rosso-antico*; most beautiful blue, in various tones down to clear gray, in *lapis lazuli*, and equally beautiful greens in *malachite*, *verd-antique* and *serpentine* marbles. Probably there is not any positively purple marble, yet there is one of the *breccia* kinds which possesses hues of that color of sufficient power to harmonize as a contrasting color, either with *giallo-antico* or *Siena*.*

On the negative side we have white, gray, and black marbles. So that by good imitations of marble, the house-painter can introduce every variety of color, naturally broken and tempered.

Marbles are imitated by various processes, but they require in the first instance a good and substantial ground-work of four or five coats of plain painting, smoothly wrought.

White-veined marble is imitated by drawing the veins with a charcoal crayon through a coat

* The only specimen I know of this marble is an antique chimney-piece at Floors Castle, the seat of his Grace the Duke of Roxburghe. It has been imitated on the columns of the telling-room and lobby of the Commercial Banking Company's premises at Edinburgh.

of wet white paint, into which they are blended with a dry brush of an oblong form made of the finest bristles, and called a marbler. When quite dry, it receives a thin coat of white-lead, ground in spirits of turpentine, and fixed by copal varnish of the finest quality, but not so strongly as to have a lustre when dry.

White marble is generally imitated wherever the stucco-work represents carving; but of all marbles it is the most difficult to imitate successfully, because it is impossible by paint to give the imitation that degree of translucency which is one of the greatest beauties of the real marble.

Siena and *giallo-antico* marbles are imitated in a somewhat similar manner. Light tints of yellow and orange-color are blended together upon an equally light ground-work, and the veins drawn through them while wet, with crayons made of colored pigments. These veins are softened into the tints by going over them lightly with the brush called the marbler, just described. When this part of the process is dry, the white crystalline specks and veins are added by means of white-lead ground in spirits of turpentine, fixed with a little copal varnish, and applied with quill feathers. When this is dry, the whole is varnished.

To imitate verd-antique and other breccia marbles, the colors are laid upon the ground-work in masses, and, while wet, they are mottled with crumpled paper, cloth, or sponge. The masses of white and black are by some artists produced by paper torn into the forms required, moistened with water, and stuck upon the ground-work, during the mottling process. This is taken off whenever that process is completed. Other artists produce these masses simply by painting them above the mottling with camel-hair pencils.

The practice of marble painters, however, is so various in respect to the imitating of these particular kinds of marble, that nothing more than the above general idea of it can be given. In all marble painting, great care should be taken to avoid the use of oil as much as possible, because it tends to change the colors and produce tawniness, so that wherever it is practicable, the vehicle ought to be a mixture of spirits of turpentine and copal varnish only. But it requires great dexterity and considerable practice to work without oil, owing to the volatility of the spirits of turpentine and the quick setting of the varnish.

ON THE VARIOUS MODES OF DECORATING THE CEILINGS AND WALLS OF DWELLING-HOUSES.

ALTHOUGH the dwelling-houses of the ancients do not seem to have been remarkable for interior comfort, yet we find, from the ruins of Pompeii and Herculaneum, that the Romans at an early period of their history were not only acquainted with the art of plastering interior walls, but also the art of rendering plaster impervious to dampness. We find from the ruins of the Alhambra and other architectural remains of the ancient Moors, that that remarkable people were likewise acquainted with these arts. (Note D.)

But in this country plastering and stucco-work seems not to have come into anything like general use, as an interior decoration, till within the last century; although we know it was introduced above three hundred years ago.

Previously to the introduction of these arts into this country, the ceilings of the apartments in our dwelling-houses generally consisted either of the boards upon which the lead-work or slating of the roof was laid with the couples which supported them, or, where one apartment was surmounted by another, of the planks which formed the floor of the latter, and the joists which supported them. In the first case, the couples, and the beams which united them, were occasionally ornamented by carving, as in Westminster Hall, and in many other ancient edifices in England, and they were occasionally further adorned by varnishing, painting, and gilding. And in the second case, the ceiling was often constructed under the joists by a framing of woodwork formed into panels, which were either filled with wood or stretched canvas. When the former was employed, the whole ceiling was often oiled or varnished, and the panels emblazoned with armorial devices; but when the panels were filled with canvas, it was painted all over, and decorated with various devices: sometimes scripture pieces, or historical subjects, were painted upon them, and specimens have been found, with subjects in which the Christian and heathen mythology are mixed. Many curious specimens of this style of decoration still exist in Scotland; perhaps the most remarkable is one in a large room at Pinkie House, the seat of Sir John Hope, Bart., which is decorated with mythological subjects and arabesque ornaments.

One of an earlier description, decorated with national devices, exists in a tolerable state of preservation in the ruins of Falkland Palace, others in some of the most ancient apartments of Holyrood Palace, and in the small room in Edinburgh Castle where James the VIth was born. A very curious specimen of this style of decoration was lately found in a house on the Castle-hill of Edinburgh, once occupied by Mary of Guise, a portion of which is preserved in the Antiquarian Museum of Edinburgh.

At this period the interior surfaces of walls were generally lined with wood framed into panels, and called wainscoting. This, in the generality of apartments, reached from the floor to the ceiling, being divided about three feet from the floor by a moulding called a surbase. This wainscoting of walls continued in use long after the introduction of plastered ceilings; and in ordinary houses was painted white, the paint being mixed with a coarse kind of varnish, made by dissolving common resin in spirits of turpentine. In the panels over the doors and chimney-piece were often introduced landscapes or other pictures, either in color, or in shades of brown or gray. When a high style of decoration was required, the whole panelling on the walls was similarly embellished, a specimen of which still remains in excellent preservation in the Council-room of George Watson's hospital near Edinburgh.

It seems the walls of the room at Pinkie House, already referred to, were decorated in a similar style with the ceiling; but the room being used as a receptacle for the wounded at the battle of Prestonpans, the painting was so disfigured, and the woodwork so injured, that the whole was removed, and plain finishing substituted.

In the mansions of the nobility this wainscoting was only carried a short way up the wall, generally from three to six feet, according to the height of the room. The space between the wainscoting and the cornice was hung either with tapestry, silk damask, or embossed leather. The manner in which tapestry and damask were hung, admitted of their being taken down for the purpose of being cleaned and aired, a process which the embossed leather did not require, as its surface was impervious to moisture and easily washed. Plastering, as already observed, was introduced into this country upwards of three hundred years ago, and in some of the early specimens it seems to have been used instead of canvas for filling in the panels of ceilings. In this manner it has been employed on the ceiling of the Chapel Royal of St James's, the panels of which are formed of wooden framework upon a plaster ground. This ceiling was painted by Holbein in 1540, and I believe is still in a state of tolerable preservation.

From that period, down to the middle of the seventeenth century, many beautiful specimens of ornamental stucco-work, in the Elizabethan style, were introduced into England, and a few into Scotland. Of the latter, there are two in excellent preservation at Winton House, the mansion of Lord Ruthven, and other two in Moray House in Edinburgh. But about the middle of the seventeenth century, a new style seems to have been introduced, of a much bolder character, composed principally of fruit, flowers, and scroll-work in high relief. Specimens of this style of decoration exist in Holyrood Palace, and in many of the mansions of the nobility and gentry throughout Scotland.

The earliest specimens of walls finished in plaster that are to be met with, seem to have been intended exclusively for painting upon, as the surface is made of an even roughness, to the same extent as the twilled canvas used in portrait painting. An excellent specimen of this style is still in good preservation in Milton House, Edinburgh. It was painted by a French artist called De la Cour, a pupil of the celebrated Watteau. Judging from existing specimens of the works of De la Cour, he seems to have been pretty largely employed by the Scottish nobility.

Plastering of ceilings and walls, with stucco ornaments in various styles, is now the almost universal mode of finishing the apartments of dwelling-houses and public buildings, and I have already observed, that the most effectual method of rendering plaster-work durable, and the apartments in which it is employed truly wholesome, is to have it thoroughly painted.

In treating of imitations of woods and marbles, I have likewise observed, regarding the painting of plastered ceilings, that when constructed in imitation of any other material, they ought also to be painted in imitation of it. When plainly finished, however, they may be painted in any way, either in tints of color or pure white. Sometimes they are finished in flatted painting of four or five coats, as already described; at others, merely primed with one or two coats, and finished in distemper color. This latter mode of finishing is more aerial in its effect than flatted painting, but not so durable.

DISTEMPER is a word derived from the French "détrempe," meaning a preparation of opaque colors ground in water, and fixed by the admixture of size, paste, or gum. Coloring plaster work in distemper, differs from fresco painting, inasmuch as the latter is applied while the plaster is quite wet, and is thereby incorporated with it, whilst the former is applied when the plaster is quite dry, and lasts only so long as the animal or vegetable substance which binds it withstands the action of the atmosphere, and this is seldom more than two years, unless when the surface of the plaster has been rendered impervious to absorption by one or two coats of paint.

Ceilings, when richly ornamented in stucco-work, are often heightened with gilding, and picked out with positive colors, as a preparation for which they must be painted in five or six coats, and flatted. The process of gilding has not yet been described, and I shall therefore give a short account of it in this place.

GILDING, as applied in decoration, is performed by the following process:—

Very fine ochre is ground in linseed oil to an impalpable paste, and then reduced to a thin consistency by the addition of more oil, and placed in a warm temperature for about twelve months, in order to render it viscid, and impart to it the property of retaining a degree of tenacity for several hours after it is dry. This is called oil gold-size, and with it all the parts intended to be gilded are painted, and will be ready to receive the gold-leaf in from twelve to eighteen hours thereafter. Gold, from its great beauty and durability, is the most valuable of all ornamental substances; but its weight and high price would render its use in decoration exceedingly limited, were it not that from its extraordinary density and malleability it may be made to cover a larger surface than an equal quantity of any other body.

The leaf gold generally used is in thickness

not more than one two hundred and eighty thousandth of an inch, but in special cases it is made thicker.

Gold leaf, from its extreme thinness, is very difficult to handle, and its proper treatment is the result of much practice and great care on the part of the workman. It is received from the manufacturer in leaves of about three inches square, which are placed between the leaves of small books, generally if not always, made from old printed paper, each of which contains twenty-five leaves, and is technically called by painters and gilders a book of gold. But the gold-beater always calculates by the thousand leaves. The leaves of these small books are rubbed with red chalk, to prevent the leaves of gold from adhering to them.

The tools by which leaf gold is applied by the decorator are a cushion, a knife, a tip, some cotton wool, and a dusting-brush. The cushion is a small thin board, the upper side of which is covered first with fine cloth, and next with thick leather with the rough side outwards; one half of the surface of the cushion is surrounded with a screen of parchment about three inches high, and on the under side of the board are fixed two pieces of leather, one to secure the thumb of the workman's left hand, upon which, while in use, it rests, and the other to receive the knife. The knife itself is about six inches long, quite straight, and having a smooth but not very sharp edge. The tip is a thin layer of camel hair, the ends of which are fixed between two cards of about three inches long, leaving about two inches of the hair free; and a dry painting-brush, called a sash-tool, answers the purpose of a duster. The decorator opens a book, and allows the leaves of the gold to fall from between those of the paper, one by one, upon the screened half of the cushion, to the number of about ten or twelve, less or more according to the work to be done, but never more than the full number contained in one book. He then takes the cushion upon the thumb of his left hand, the tip between the same thumb and fore-finger, and the knife in his right hand; upon the point of the latter he lifts a leaf of gold from the screened end of the cushion, and flattens it on the other end by blowing gently upon it. He then cuts it with the gold-knife into such pieces as the work requires, takes the tip between the fore-finger and thumb of his right hand, placing the knife between those of the left, and with the former he lifts the pieces of gold-leaf from the cushion and lays them upon the parts which have been painted with the gold-size. The hair of the tip is made slightly tenacious by being drawn through the hair of the head, and thus it easily lifts the gold-leaf from the cushion. This is called oil-gilding, in contradistinction to burnished and mat gilding, and is the only kind practised by the house-painter. It is washable, and when properly done, will last for upwards of a century.

When the stucco enrichments on ceilings and cornices are heightened with gilding they are sometimes, but not so often as they ought to be, picked out with positive colors. There is no branch of the painter's art that requires more care and judgment than this. If the colors be used in their full intensity, crudity and harshness are likely to be the result. Tempering and balancing are as much required in the mixing and arranging of the colors upon a picked-out ceiling, as they are in the mixing and arranging of those employed in a picture. These colors are greatly improved, and have much the appearance and quality of fresco painting, by being reduced from their dry state to paint by spirits of turpentine only, and fixed by the admixture of a little of the finest copal. When mixed of ordinary oil-colors they are almost certain to change, and to become heavy in their effect; but, treated as I have described, they never change. Their proper management, however, both in the mixing and laying on, requires care and experience.

I now come to the various modes of decorating the plastered walls of our ordinary apartments; of which modes there are two now in general use, namely, painting and paper-hanging. Having already made the reader acquainted with the former, I shall now give some account of the latter.

Paper-Hangings were, I believe, first imported into Britain from China, and next from France, and still continue to be imported from both those countries. They were begun to be manufactured in this country about two hundred years ago, at first in a very rude style, but latterly with more care and refinement, though much still remains to be done by our paper-stainers to raise the art to that degree of excellence to which it has been brought in France. Paper-hangings were first used in imitation of, or as a cheap substitute for the tapestry or damask previously in use, and were glued to coarse canvas, and stretched upon the wall in a similar manner to those more expensive fabrics—hence the name paper-hangings. Now, however, the paper is fixed to the plaster by means of glue and paste; a solution of the former being applied to the plaster, and the back of the paper being thickly coated with the latter. There are various kinds of paper-hangings manufactured in this country, all of which are made in pieces of twelve yards long. The cheapest are made of coarse papers, colored in the pulp like blotting paper, but of various tints, and upon this a pattern of a uniform color is printed, in distemper, by a stamp used in the hand, or by a cylinder.

The next kind, and that which is in most general use, is made of various qualities of cartridge-paper, upon which a solid flat ground of distemper is laid, and the pattern stamped upon it either by machinery or by the hand. According to the quality of the cartridge paper and groundwork, as also the number of times it must go through the stamping process to produce the various tints and shading of the pattern, is the price of this kind of paper-hanging regulated. The next class is composed of those that have satin grounds, the lustre of which is produced by friction. These grounds are often embossed with patterns, some of which represent watered silk, and others a flowered or striped pattern; upon this a colored pattern is printed in distemper, in the same way as upon the plain grounds. This class of paper hangings is of all others the best, as it is the most impervious to the absorption of moisture from the atmosphere—the most easily cleaned, and, decidedly, the most durable. The next highest priced paper is that called flocked paper, which is produced by the pattern being stamped on any description of groundwork with japan gold-size, and dyed wool minced into powder shaken over it while the pattern is still wet. This woollen powder, which is called flock, then adheres to the japan gold-size which forms the figure of the pattern. When this is dry the loose flock is dusted off, and the pattern is generally enriched by the application of additional blocks, with color or dry, in which latter case the flock receives an impression which considerably enhances its effect. The next class are those in which the pattern is either wholly or partially produced by metal: the metal is either applied in powder, in the same manner as flock, or in leaves like those of gold. This metallic powder is bisulphurate of tin, and the leaf metal is made of fine copper, or a mixture of copper with zinc, tin, or some other metal that will give it more the color of gold than when in its native state. These metals are often added to colored and flocked patterns. Paper-hangings upon which leaf metal is employed, are much more expensive than those done with the metallic powder; but the leaf kind has much greater brilliancy, and is more durable than the other.

Having endeavored to make the reader acquainted with the nature of the covering which a plastered wall receives from the operations of the painter, when the proper materials and workmanship are applied, I shall now attempt to explain the nature of that which the paper-hanger's art affords. Let us take, for example, what is termed a body-ground paper—one of those sold at from three to five shillings a piece of twelve lineal yards, which are equal, when hung, to little more than six superficial square yards of painting, and examine the nature of the clothing which the wall has received when the operation of hanging it has been completed.

The first part of the process, as already noticed, is to give the plaster upon which the paper is to be fixed, a coat of size: this is an animal substance, liable to be softened by the humidity of the atmosphere, and to consequent putrefaction. Above this we have the thick coating of paste by which the paper is fastened to the plaster This paste is a vegetable substance, also liable to be softened by dampness, and consequently subject to mildew and rot. The paper itself is composed of a pulp made from hemp, or cotton rags, hardened by size, and it is therefore likewise easily softened by moisture, and subject to putrefaction and mildew; while the distemper-color which forms the pattern and its ground-work, is, like all that is under it, easily softened by absorbing the humidity of the atmosphere. Now, I dare say most of my readers may have occasionally met with writing-paper, the odor of which was very unpleasant, and when they reflect that this odor always arises from the size used in hardening the paper, having become putrid from dampness, they will easily comprehend what effect the moisture from the atmosphere must have upon a papered wall where so much size has been necessarily employed. Although most people know how easily paper mildews when kept damp for a few days, and that the exhalations from putrid animal substances and mildewed vegetable substances are both very unwholesome; yet few seem to reflect that this unwholesomeness may arise from the improper use of paper-hangings on the interior walls of their dwellings.

In bed-rooms and drawing-rooms, into which the external air is not necessarily admitted, unless in dry weather, and in which the temperature is kept pretty uniform, no injurious effect may take place from the use of paper-hangings, especially with respect to those that are satin-grounded; yet it is often found, in removing old paper from the walls of such apartments, that there are considerable masses of rottenness and mildew between it and the plaster. This may very generally arise from accidental dampness, and in some cases may be accounted for by the apartment being long unoccupied, and not properly secured against the effects of atmospheric dampness. The ancient mode of using paper upon canvas was much preferable to what is now practised, because they formed together but a thin body, which could not absorb much dampness from the atmosphere, and would dry rapidly on a fire being lighted in the apartment; whereas plaster is often put on a brick partition, about a foot thick, which, on any natural change in the temperature of the atmosphere from coolness to warmth, will continue to absorb moisture until its whole mass rises to the same temperature as the atmosphere itself. In Scotland, we often find this humidity condensing upon the painted walls of our lobbies, staircases, corridors, and passages, until it accumulates upon the surface to such an extent as to run down in streams upon the floors and steps. Now, in the case of the walls of such apartments being papered, all this accumulation of moisture is absorbed, and must afterwards be given out, combined with the effluvia from the decayed animal and vegetable substances necessarily employed in this mode of decoration. Painting is, therefore, decidedly preferable to papering in lobbies, staircases, corridors, and passages, both in point of wholesomeness and durability, the more especially as they cannot be kept at so equal a temperature as the apartments to which they lead, and to which they are the reservoirs of air in bad weather and during the night, whilst all other inlets are closed. Neither is paper a good decoration for the walls of a dining-room, because it absorbs the steams from the table, which must be again given out along with the effluvia of the substances already described. The quantity given out, as the absorbed moisture evaporates from a papered wall, may be so small as not to make any perceptible impression upon the sense of smell; but that it must, to some extent, contaminate the atmosphere of the apartment, while it continues to be given out, cannot be denied. The prepossession in favor of paper-hanging has doubtless arisen from its producing an apparently clothed and warm effect to the eye, as also from the gayety and cheerfulness that it is capable of imparting at a smaller cost than any other mode of decoration. And certainly for bed-rooms, where the disadvantages to which I have alluded are not so likely to be felt, these qualities give it a preference. Satin-grounds, however, should always be preferred to body-grounds for bed-room papers, as they are not only the most wholesome, but, from their greater durability, are ultimately the cheapest.

In respect to the walls of drawing-rooms, there are many styles of decoration equally as suitable as paper-hangings in producing the effects of gayety, cheerfulness, and grandeur, and at a cost not exceeding that of the generality of gilded and flocked paper-hangings so employed; while, taking into consideration the much greater durability of the painting, such styles of decoration prove ultimately to be less than half the expense of papering. Such of those styles of decoration as I have been for the last twenty years in the habit of practising, and such as I have more recently invented, I shall endeavor to describe.

STIPPLED FLAT-PAINTING AND GOLD.—The process of stippled flat-painting has already been described, and its great durability and real comfort commented on. Upon this kind of painting, whatever the tint may be, the gilded pattern is produced by the following process:—

The outline of the pattern is first drawn upon paper, and closely pricked with a needle. This paper is called a pounce, and when the paint is quite dry, it is laid upon the wall, and rubbed over with a bag of powdered charcoal, which, going through the pricked outline, leaves an impression of it upon the wall. The pattern is generally confined within a few superficial square feet, and of course the process is repeated until the whole wall is covered. The decorative artists then proceed to paint the pattern on the wall with oil gold-size, and afterwards to apply the gold-leaf by the process already fully described. Some patterns are so simple that the gold-size may be applied by a stencil; that is, cutting the pattern out of very thin pasteboard, or painted paper, and laying this cut-out paper on the wall, and applying the gold-size through it with a largeish brush. The most simple patterns are composed of stars, rosettes, or sprigs, and sometimes of a mixture of two of those, placed at intervals of from ten to twenty inches apart, according to the size of the room, or taste of the employer. The richer patterns are made occasionally to embody some of the devices of the armorial bearings of the proprietors of the mansion, or monograms of their initial letters, surrounded by rosettes, and united by festoons and sprigs. Indeed, there is such ample latitude for variety of pattern, that the decorator need not necessarily, in the course of many years' practice, make two drawing-rooms exactly the same in this respect. The stippling of the groundwork imparts great richness to the gilding, and prevents the tinselled glare that is produced by gilding on a plain surface.

Imitation of Gold Embroidery.—This is the richest style of gilded decoration applied to drawing-room walls, and the following is the process: The walls are painted four or five coats in the usual way, and allowed to harden; they then receive a coat of very thick tenacious paint, of which bees-wax and gum-mastic are ingredients. While this coat is wet, a fine toothed ivory graining-comb is drawn through it, first diagonally down from right to left, then from left to right, and lastly in a vertical direction. By this process the appearance of cloth composed of strong threads is produced upon the wall. This thick coating requires eight or ten days to harden, even in warm weather. When it is quite hard it receives a coat of flat paint, of any tint that may be chosen, which prevents the impression made by the comb from being very distinct at a little distance. The outline of the pattern is produced above this by a pounce, and is gold-sized and gilded in the usual way. It will now be found that the effect of the light reflected from the points of the granules that are gilded gives the pattern the appearance of being wrought in thread of gold.*

DECORATIVE BORDERING.—This style is equally suitable to either dining-rooms or drawing-rooms, and admits of great variety. It consists of painted and gilded borders being made to surround the apartment at top and bottom of the wall, and occasionally, where the room is uniform in its divisions, they are carried round the angles also; by which latter mode of application each side and end of the room is thrown into a panel. It is generally found requisite to show an inch or two of the ground color of the wall, between the border and the cornice, in order to prevent any diminution in the apparent height of the apart-

* This style of decoration has been executed with great effect upon a pure white ground, in one of the largest, and finest drawing-rooms in the neighborhood of Edinburgh. The pattern was composed of festoons of laurel, with a monogram of the family name.

ment. These borders are sometimes bounded by a straight line, and at others broken into the wall, and end upon it in light tendrils.

They may either be composed entirely of gilding, entirely of colors, or of a combination of the two. The ground-work of the wall may either be plain, or have a pattern. The color introduced into these borders is very generally that of the curtains, but the richest and most beautiful effect is produced by a judicious mixture of various colors and gilding.

There has lately been introduced a new style of bordering, applicable principally to drawing-rooms where pictures are hung, and consisting in the greater part of the wall being finished in stippled flatted-painting,* of a grave tone of color, and the decoration confined to a pendant ornament, proceeding two or three feet from the cornice, and either finished simply in gilding, or in a mixture of gilding with rich coloring.*

* This novel style of decoration was suggested to me by an employer of a highly cultivated mind and excellent taste, and executed in his house in Edinburgh. The effect was everything that could be desired, both as regarded the pictures and general appearance of the rooms. The color was a warm hue of green.

The PATENT IMITATION OF DAMASK is another style of painting suitable for any apartment in a dwelling-house, and is remarkable for its great durability and cleanliness, every successive washing improving its effect. For this style of painting I obtained a patent in 1826, and the apartments, upon the walls of which it was first applied, are still as perfect as when newly finished. It resembles flocked paper; but it is as superior to it in appearance, as it is in cleanliness and durability. On account of these latter qualities, it is the best of all modes of decoration for the walls of a dining-room. I have already observed that paper is not a good covering for the walls of a dining-room, in consequence of its liability to absorb the moisture from the breath of the company and the steam of the dishes, which it is well known must again be given out as the atmosphere of the room begins to cool, along with a certain portion of the effluvia from the animal and vegetable substances already described. Now, on a painted wall this moisture condenses on the surface, and a current of fresh air will rapidly dry it off, while occasional washing will remove any residuum that may accumulate from the evaporation of this moisture. In the patent imitation of damask, these advantages are combined with a clothed and comfortable appearance to the eye.

There are two processes by which the patent imitation of damask is produced upon plastered walls. The first is by thoroughly painting the plaster in four or five coats, then outlining a pattern upon it in black-lead, and coating it over with a thick substance composed of oil, mastic varnish, bees-wax, sugar-of-lead, umber, or other coloring pigments, and making an impression on this with an iron comb while it is wet The impression of the comb is then obliterated upon the pattern by the thick substance being smoothed upon it with a camel-hair pencil; the whole, when quite dry, is then painted over with any color, and varnished with copal.

The other method is that now almost uniformly adopted. The plaster is, as in the first process, thoroughly painted, and the outline of the pattern impressed upon it by means of a pounce; this outline is filled in with the thick tenacious substance already mentioned, which, however, may now be made opaque by the introduction of white lead. Fine pit or sea sand is prepared by drying and sifting, and while the tenacious substance with which the pattern has been painted remains wet, the sand is thrown against the wall with some force until the pattern be all covered with it; when this is quite dry, which will be in the course of a few days, all the loose sand is carefully brushed off, leaving only what adheres firmly to the tenacious substance of which the pattern is formed. The whole is now carefully painted over with a coat of flatted paint of the same color as the ground-work. The process by which these two kinds of imitation damask are produced, although different, are the same in principle,—that is, the effect of damask is given by means of the combination of a rough and a smooth surface only, without any variety of tint or shade.

IMITATION MOROCCO is another excellent style of painting very suitable for either libraries or dining-rooms. It is, like the varnished imitation of damask, produced by laying upon a thoroughly painted wall a coat of thick tenacious paint, and giving it the peculiar effect of the surface of morocco, by means of a toothed instrument made either of ivory or steel, and finishing it with another coat of paint, and one of varnish.

There are many other styles and processes by which the walls of dwelling-houses and public buildings may be decorated by the painter; but what I have here given are the most practically useful, and, while they are not more costly than paper-hangings of equal appearance, have the advantages of greater cleanliness and durability

NOTES.

NOTE A. p. 52.

A correspondent of "*The Fine Arts Journal,*" (No. X p. 171.) referring to an article that appeared in No. V. of the same journal, has treated the subject of the power of music, in conveying a meaning, independently of its being accompanied by words, in so masterly a manner, that I shall give his letter entire:—

"I much regret the paper on the Descriptive Power of Music, in your 5th number, has not met with an answer from more competent hands than mine, which I was in hopes would have been the case, and had forgotten the subject until in your last appeared an assumption that the argument was proved, than which there never was a greater error. In that paper it is stated, that 'if an individual were asked what he meant by *so descriptive,* unless the said piece of music was of itself described —for instance, as the Pastoral Symphony, or the many overtures to operas, which of course are intended to have reference to the opera itself—he would answer by commencing *de novo,* the same string of epithets; being totally unable to say what was the music described, or what it was even characteristic of. This is not put forward as a mere statement, but as a fact'

"I doubt the fact, but if true, it cannot affect the question: because we do not go to hear music for the sake of adapting words to all we hear, and are not therefore prepared to class and express our ideas on the moment, or even on once hearing When the term *so descriptive,* is used, the meaning is, that words could with facility be adapted to the music from its capacity to continue any course of *ideas* to which it may give rise in the mind If it is required of music to convey *facts and substances*, more is demanded than even language can offer, without that most convenient word, conventionalism.

"A slow or quick time has a different effect on the nervous system where no conventionalism exist, and no difference of habit could alter the effect. It might just as well be said, that being intoxicated by a strong liquor was only a conventionalism, and that if we had accustomed ourselves to get drunk on water it would have become an highly intoxicating beverage, and that we might have drank whiskey-toddy by the gallon without its having any effect on the nervous system.

"The color for mourning does not affect the mind of the observer who feels not sorrow for the person in black: it is not intended, and does not influence the feelings, without knowledge of the parties.

"The person in black frequently only professes grief or respect for those gone, nor are the colors used in different countries by religious sects intended to excite your feelings, otherwise than by indicating the rank the wearer holds in society, and that he claims personally a due share of respect. The particular color in none of these cases is supposed to arise from or evidence the idea, it is only a livery of rank or condition. Admitting the laws regulating the harmony of color and sound are the same, C. J. fails in any way to connect them with his subject

"'A sound *per se*, or succession of sounds, conveys no idea but a noise,—*agreeable or otherwise, as the case may be*' Now, without noticing these last words, which admit the whole question, we will force it out of the first part—a noise You are awoke in the night by a noise—nothing follows. Is not the suspense productive of terror? The noise is repeated Let it be what it will, it conveys to your mind something. it is descriptive of some action or accident

"A single blast from a trumpet *is a noise;* true, and several blasts *may be* a greater noise. I have heard such where they should not have been; but a succession of sounds *may* be a production of an effect. Let C. J produce the following to any uninitiated person, and ask if these chords have no effect on the mind of his listeners, even on the pianoforte He need not try it on the instruments for which he knows it is written; and if even separately from its story, from all that may be supposed to convey any intention, let him say whether it does not affect the minds of his hearers, with sensations producing ideas If so, it is descriptive; no matter, though the impression be different in each hearer, it is still descriptive * Here is but a portion of a sentence, a word, a syllable, doing all that is deemed possible. The error is in calling on the mind of any one hearing a symphony to put a story or description to what has been heard without reflection or re-hearing. We do not go to hear music for the purpose of adapting words, and hence are not able to do so on their being demanded from us, nor am I aware that any one person has ever indulged the idea in public. It is in some measure a novelty that would, I am sure, be productive of much gratification; so different is my opinion to that of your correspondent. To put a story or description to what the mind has heard for the first time would be very difficult; though I have heard a leader with a lively imagination improvise, and continue a single story throughout a whole symphony of Haydn. On first hearing a portion of Rossini's *Stabat Mater*, without a knowledge of the meaning of the words or the intention, it forcibly impressed me as such as angels might chant in praise of the Deity, and that music of such pretension had never been presented to me in all I had before heard, the most elevated still falling short of what the mind demanded. Here was the abstract idea, true evidence of character only. On being again presented to the mind, if amplification ensued, that would be evidence of its being descriptive; no matter if, as before stated, different individuals thought differently on the subject—a ship is to you or to me a ship; to others the same

* We are unable to insert the music, but it will be sufficient for our musical readers that the passage is from the part of the Commendatore in *Don Giovanni*, to the works "*Don Giovanni, a cenar teco m'invitasti et son venuto.*'

would be a barque, a brig, a schooner, this being a defect in our knowledge, not in the ship itself: and all who make nothing but a noise out of the above chords, may justly doubt their own capacity to judge of more complicated or more lengthened portions of musical productions

"In this argument we have nothing to do with pieces that have had words adapted.

"They are by its nature totally inadmissible: if wishy-washy without them, it can only prove an inefficient composer or author in each particular case; but has no reference to the question at issue.

"But the pieces without number of the three composers cited, that have no ideas at present attached to them by authority that will come within the generally accepted term, 'so descriptive,' will enable any of your readers to test this question, and, in the full hope that some one of them will do so, and favor you with merely an abstract, I leave the question thus to be decided by others, confident of the result.

"If we consider this more philosophically, if we inquire and define what a sensation is, and how the mind is acted upon by external objects to produce sensations of pain or pleasure, we shall be coming more to the marrow of the question, and this shall be done, if the position cannot be demonstrated without it, on a future occasion, if you will favor me with the space.—I am yours, &c. G."

NOTE B, p. 132

IN one of the most wealthy and populous cities in Scotland, the journeymen, in memorializing their masters, commence as follows:—

"PAINTERS' HALL, —— —— 8th May.

"We beg leave, most respectfully, to intimate, that at a general meeting of the journeymen painters, held within the society's hall, on Monday evening the 6th instant, it was unanimously resolved—'That we respectfully bring under your notice a few of the grievances at present existing in the trade.' . . .

Amongst the numerous evils of which we have to complain, we beg leave to submit the following:—

"First, it is a notorious fact that a number of employers in this city have, for a long period, been in the practice of taking into their employment an unlimited number of half-bred and run-away apprentices, young men who are quite incompetent to execute any part of our work in a satisfactory manner. Such a system is prone to innumerable evils; inasmuch that it has been the cause of a great portion of the public sending to a considerable distance (Edinburgh, &c.) for painters to execute their work."

"The second evil is of a very serious nature, not only to us but to the public generally; that is, the too frequent and abundant use of size to all kinds of painting work, which most unjustly deprives us of labor, our only inheritance, at the same time dealing unjustly to the public, your only support. There are so many glaring proofs before us of this evil, that were it made known to the public, the consequences would be most serious to those parties adopting such nefarious practices—a system against which no honest employer can compete, and which will be put down at all hazards."

This memorial not being satisfactorily received by the master painters, a bill, upwards of two feet long, and about a foot and a half broad, was posted throughout the city in question stating that

"The journeymen painters of ——— have for a long time viewed with astonishment and indignation the nefarious system which several of the master painters of ——— have adopted in the execution of painting—a system of fraud unparalleled in the history of any trade. We have hitherto allowed the practice to continue, in the hope that the public would find out the disgraceful manner in which their work has been executed; but the evil, instead of being detected, is progressing to an enormous extent. So indiscriminate is the application, that from the drawing-room to the kitchen, the pernicious article of SIZE is substituted for OIL PAINT.

"To give some idea to non-professionals of the manner in

which this system operates, it will be necessary to enter into detail—

"1st, Estimates wherein work is to receive *four coats* is thus schemed: A coat of strong size is first applied to the whole, it then gets the first coat of paint; another coat of size follows. The second and third coat of paint is then put on, which finishes it. Here, it is seen, a full coat of paint is saved on the walls and other parts which come more immediately under inspection; and when it is taken into account that cornices are never hit in, backs of shutters, presses, &c. receiving but *two coats*, it will be found to be a very profitable system to the dishonest employer.

"2d Estimates for three-coat work It receives a coat of full-strength size, another coat of reduced size, mixed with whiting; it then receives its first coat of paint; another coat of reduced size, called clear cole, prepares it for varnish; but if it be finished in flat, the clear cole is not necessary. Here, again, the system is carried out on work that the three coats, if all put on, would not be sufficient to make a proper and durable job. But it is on work intended for imitations that the WHOLESALE SYSTEM OF PLUNDER IS CARRIED OUT. For example, take a dining-room, which should get three coats for oak (walls, ceiling, and wood-work); it receives a coat of full-strength size another coat of reduced size, mixed with whiting; it then gets a coat of round color, which furnishes it for the grainer. Now, we ask, if parties who adopt this wholesale system of plunder are worthy of public patronage?

"We would caution the public to be careful of whom they employ, for the system has arrived at such a pitch that it would require CONSTANT WATCHING to prevent the use of SIZE and ADULTERATED LEAD."

In respect to the workmen employed, the bill gave a list of ten establishments, employing in all 158 hands, 71 of whom were journeymen, and 87 were apprentices.

Whether these accusations were true, to the extent here assumed, or whether they have been as yet contradicted by any of the parties against whom they were so publicly brought forward, I do not know, but that a system of the kind does prevail in other cities, as well as that in which this meeting took place, there can be no doubt, and it is but just to the more respectable portion of the profession that every opportunity should be taken to make the public acquainted with the fact.

NOTE C, p. 142

SUCH was the opinion of the celebrated Author of Waverley. Mr Lockhart, in his life of that great man, observes, "In the painting of the interior too, Sir Walter, personally directed everything. He abominated the common-place daubing of walls, panels, doors, and window-boards, with coats of white, blue, or gray, and thought that sparklings and edgings of gilding only made their baldness and poverty more noticeable. He desired to have about him, wherever he could manage it, rich, though not gaudy hangings, or substantial old-fashioned wainscot work, with no ornament but that of carving, and where the wood was to be painted at all, it was done in strict imitation of oak or cedar. Except in the drawing-room, which he abandoned to Lady Scott's taste, all the roofs were in appearance of antique carved oak, relieved by coats of arms duly blazoned at the intersections of the beams, and resting on cornices, to the eye of the same material, but really composed of casts of plaster of Paris"—(*Life of Sir Walter Scott*, vol. v. p 323.)

Sir Walter certainly did, as Mr. Lockhart observes, direct every thing personally, connected with the building and decoration of his mansion, and it remains to this day not the least interesting and remarkable creation of his wonderful mind.

It is now upwards of twenty-seven years since I had the honor of receiving the orders of Sir Walter regarding the decoration of the first part of Abbotsford House that was built. These orders, which were given on the eve of his leaving for London to receive his baronetcy, were of too important a nature, and given in too remarkable a manner, not to leave an indelible impression on the mind of one so ready to devote his best energies to their execution. Every thing connected with the memory of that great man being full of interest, I trust I shall be excused, for here giving a few reminiscences, of what passed on that occasion, and during the progress of the decorations at Abbotsford.

The first stipulation made by Sir Walter was, that, as he would be absent during the whole progress of the work, which he required should be finished by his return to Scotland, I should remain with the workmen upon the spot, and superintend it personally, in order that the directions he had given me (which were all verbal), should be strictly followed. He ordered me to paint the dining-room ceiling, cornice, niches, &c. in imitation of oak to match the doors, window-shutters, and wainscoting, which were made of that wood; to emblazon some small shields in the bosses of the ceiling, with their heraldic metals and colors, and to fix four pictures on certain parts of the wall, namely, one of a lady (called the flower of Yarrow), over the chimney-piece, another, a portrait of General Fairfax, on the centre of the opposite side of the room, and two small ones over the doors, one of which, if I recollect rightly, was a view of the ruins of Melrose Abbey by moonlight. These, after being fixed to the wall by a narrow moulding of oak, were to be surrounded with an imitation of a carved frame of the same material, painted in light and shade upon the flat plaster To cover the remainder of the wall he gave me an Indian paper of a crimson color, with a small gilded pattern upon it. This paper he said he did not altogether approve of for a dining-room, but as he had got it in a present expressly for that purpose, and as he believed it to be rare, he would have it put upon the room, rather than hurt the feelings of the donor. I observed to Sir Walter, that there would scarcely be enough to cover the whole remainder of the wall after the pictures were fixed up, to which he replied, that in that case I might paint the recess for the sideboard in imitation of oak The small armory adjoining, he directed to be painted altogether in imitation of oak, as also the wood-work of his library and staircase; the walls of the former being painted a plain color of a quiet tone, and those of the latter and passages, in imitation of stone-work. The decoration of the bed-rooms, and painting of the servants' apartments were left to be ordered by Lady Scott.

Most of my readers will be aware that the mansion-house of Abbotsford was built in two distinct portions—a period of four years elapsing between the completion of the first and that of the second The first part consisted of the present dining-room, the present breakfast parlor, which was then Sir Walter's library and study, and in which many of the celebrated novels were written,—the small armory entering from the dining-room, with the bed-rooms and attics above these apartments This was the portion of the mansion to which the orders I have mentioned related, and the accommodation of which were eked out by what remained of the original small house that stood upon the property. These orders I received early in March 1820, and with eight assistants commenced their execution on the 20th of that month, and had the whole finished by the end of April, as agreed.

The recess for the sideboard, at the end of the dining-room, had at first been finished in imitation of oak, but finding that there was a sufficient quantity of paper to cover this as well as the other parts of the wall, I had it put on above the painting, in the belief that Sir Walter had agreed to the painting of it merely as an alternative, arising from the supposed want of paper In giving his orders regarding the painting of the staircase and lobby he made no allusion to the steps of the one, or floor of the other; and as there were no floorcloth or stair carpeting ordered I had them painted in imitation of marble, the floor of the lobby being in the figure of an ornamental pavement

Sir Walter returned to Scotland about the end of April, and either before going to Edinburgh, or soon thereafter, visited Abbotsford. He arrived in the evening, and had no sooner put his foot upon the painted pavement of the lobby than he observed, "I surely did not order this to be done." I then explained to him that as no orders had been given for any other covering to the bare stones, I had taken the liberty of painting them; he replied that he did not so much object to the painting, as to the making of imitation joints crossing the real ones, and good-naturedly added, that he believed the stones themselves would rise up in evidence against the impropriety of such a proceeding. And so it literally turned out; for in less than two years the true joints of the pavement, notwithstanding all my labor to conceal them by puttying and polishing, began to show themselves, intersecting most awkwardly those false joints by which I had endeavored to imitate an ornamental arrangement of marble slabs. On entering the dining-room he had no sooner expressed his satisfaction with the general effect, than the papered recess in which the sideboard stood attracted his attention; and he asked if it had not been agreed that it should be painted in imitation of oak. When I explained how it came to be papered, he said it was all right, but that he heartily wished the paper had fallen short as I had at first anticipated, for having seen in some ancient houses in England these recesses fitted up in real oak, he was convinced it was the proper style. I did not mention to Sir Walter at this time that the recess had been painted in imitation of oak before the paper was put upon it, in case the taking of it off might destroy the painting, and put the room for some time in an unfit state to receive company, which would not then have suited Sir Walter's arrangements. In the morning, however, I examined the state of the painting, and finding it quite good underneath the paper, had two of my most expert workmen employed in removing that covering from its surface without Sir Walter's knowledge, so that when he came down to breakfast the recess was completely finished in imitation of oak frame-work instead of being covered with crimson paper, as he had seen it the night before In casting his eyes round the room, he immediately observed, "I must surely have dreamt that that recess was papered like the rest of the wall, although the recollection of having seen it so is too vivid, and too much mixed up with other facts for me to believe it a dream—it is like enchantment. —How has it been changed in so short a time?" The matter was then explained, and he was highly pleased.

The plans for the second and greater portion of the mansion were, as the former plans had been, supplied by Mr. Blore the architect, of London, from Sir Walter's own suggestions, given verbally while there in 1820 These plans comprised the great entrance-hall, the library, the drawing-room, the study, and the small oratory, with additional bed-rooms above, and accommodation for servants below these apartments; and the execution of the work was commenced early in 1821.

The great interest that Sir Walter took in the building and decorating of this part of his mansion, and his knowledge of the subject, are strongly evinced in his letters to his friend Mr. Daniel Terry, the actor, who, being resident in London at the time, seems to have rendered him considerable assistance Mr T. seems also to have engaged Mr. Atkinson, another London architect, to carry out Sir Walter's ideas in respect to the details of the plaster work, wood finishing, &c of the interior.

In a letter to Mr T, dated Abbotsford, November 10th, 1822, he says—"I got all the plans safe, and they are delightful The library ceiling will be superb, and we have plenty of ornaments for it without repeating one of those in the eating-room . . . I have had three grand hawls since I last wrote to you The pulpit, repentance-stool, King's-seat, and God knows how much of carved wainscot, from the Kirk of Dunfermline, enough to coat the hall to the height of seven feet,—supposing it boarded above, for hanging guns, old portraits intermixed with armor, &c. It will be a superb entrance gallery: this is hawl the first. Hawl the second is twenty-four pieces of the most splendid Chinese paper, twelve feet high by four wide, a present from my cousin Hugh Scott, enough to finish the drawing-room and two bed-rooms Hawl third is a quantity of what is called Jamaica cedar-wood, enough for fitting up both the drawing-room and the library, including the presses, shelves, &c.: the wood is finely pencilled, and most beautiful, something like the color of gingerbread; it costs very little more than oak, works much easier, and is never touched by vermin of any kind. I sent Mr. Atkinson a specimen, but it was from the plain end of the plank. the interior is finely veined and variegated. Your kind and unremitting exertions in our favor will soon plenish the drawing-room. Thus we at present stand. We have a fine old English cabinet, with China &c ,—and two superb elbow-chairs, the gift of Constable, carved most magnificently, with groups of children, fruits, and flowers, in the Italian taste: they came from Rome, and are much admired. It seems to me that the mirror you mention, being framed in carved box, would answer admirably well with the chairs, which are of the same material. The mirror should, I presume, be placed over the drawing-room chimney-piece, and opposite to it I mean to put an antique table of mozaic marbles, to support Chantrey's bust. A good sofa would be desirable, and so would the tapestry screen, if really fresh and beautiful; but as much of our furniture will be a little antiquated, one would not run too much into that taste in so small an apartment For the library I have the old oak chairs now in the little armory, eight in number, and might add one or two pair of the ebony chairs you mention. I should think this enough, for many seats in such a room must impede access to the books; and I don't mean the library to be on ordinary occasions a public room Perhaps the tapestry-screen would suit better here than in the drawing-room. I have one library-table here, and shall have another made for atlases and prints. For the hall I have four chairs of black-oak In other matters we can make it out well enough. In fact it is my object rather to keep under my new accommodations at first, both to avoid immediate outlay, and that I may leave room for pretty things that may occur hereafter. I would to Heaven I could take a cruise with you through the brokers, which would be the pleasantest affair possible, only I am afraid I should make a losing voyage of it Mr Atkinson has missed a little my idea of the oratory, fitting it up entirely as a book-case, whereas, I should like to have had recesses for curiosities, for the Bruce's skull, for a Crucifix, &c. &c.—in short, a little cabinet, instead of a book-closet. Four sides of books would be perfectly sufficient; the other four, so far as not occupied by door or window, should be arranged tastefully for antiquities, &c., like the inside of an antique cabinet—with drawers, and shottles, and funny little arches. The oak screen dropped as from the clouds; it is most acceptable, I might have guessed there was only one kind friend so ready to supply hay to my hobby-horse You have my views in these matters and your own taste; and I will send the *needful* when you apprise me of the amount total. Where things are not quite satisfactory, it is better to wait a while on every account, for the amusement is over when one has room for nothing more"

In regard to the carved oak from the Kirk at Dumfermline, it did not turn out so useful as Sir Walter thought it would. The pulpit was, if I recollect rightly, circular, and some other difficulties arose during the progress of the carpenters' work, in its application to the wainscoting of the entrance-hall A further supply was therefore required, and upon this subject Sir Walter wrote to me from Abbotsford, asking me if I knew of anything of the kind in Edinburgh that could be purchased at a moderate price. At that time there were no shops in Edinburgh, such as those where old oak carvings can now be so easily obtained—for I believe Sir Walter Scott's adoption of these articles as a decoration, gave the first impulse to that rage for them which has since existed, and which is now so well responded to by all who deal in other antiquities This letter brought to my recollection that at the door of a house that stood (and still stands) in a wood-yard at the foot of Wariston's close, in the High Street, there was a white painted porch with carved panels, the figures upon which used, long before, to be a subject of admiration to me and other boys attending a school in the neighborhood I therefore called upon the owner, and obtained permission to examine it. Upon doing so, I found it was made of oak, and that the figures in the panels were allegorical of the cardinal virtues, &c. The owner of these panels told me that there were originally twelve of them; but having found that eight were sufficient for his porch, he had sold the other four to a friend who had fitted them up as the doors of an inclosed bed. He told me also that he had purchased them, with some other old wood, in the neighborhood of Holyrood Palace, in one of the apartments of which they had originally formed the decoration of a portion of the wall. He agreed to let me have those in his possession for as much money as would cover the expense of putting up a new porch to his house, the amount of which he was to ascertain, and at the same time gave me the address of the party who had purchased the other four. When I acquainted Sir Walter with those particulars, giving him at the same time a sketch of the panelling, with its dimensions, he immediately replied, authorizing the purchase of it, as also of that portion which the original proprietor had parted with, as the panels were in size, shape, and style the very thing he required for the completion of the wainscoting of the entrance-hall; and desired to know as soon as possible whether I had succeeded in procuring the whole or only the portion which formed the porch; "For," he added, "we must cut our coat according to our cloth; and if we only get the porch we must then just stretch our leather as much as we can" The whole was at last purchased, and now forms a principal part of the wainscoting of the entrance-hall

I now regret having parted with the letters I received from Sir Walter at this time, and during the progress of the decorations; but they were all given to friends who collected autographs, as I did not then consider that I should ever have again to refer to them

Again, in January, 1823, he writes to Mr Terry, as follows: "I am first to report progress, for your consideration and Mr Atkinson's, of what I have been doing here. Everything about the house has gone *à pieu mieux*, and the shell is completely finished, all the upper story and garrets, as well as the basement, have had their first coat of plaster, being first properly fenced from the exterior air. The only things which we now greatly need are the designs for ceilings of the hall and drawing-room, as the smiths and plasterers are impatient for their working plans, the want of which rather stops them"—(*Life*, vol v. p 238) Again, in the same letter, he says.—"I am completely Lady Wishfort as to the escritoire. In fact my determination would very much depend on the possibility of showing it to advantage; for if it be such as is set up against a wall, like what is called, *par excellence*, a writing-desk, you know we have no space in the library that is not occupied by book-presses. If, on the contrary, it stands quite free, why, I do not know—I must e'en leave it to you to decide between taste and prudence. The silk damask, I fancy, we must have for the drawing-room curtains; those in the library we shall have of superfine crimson cloth from Galashiels, made of mine own wool I should like the silk to be sent down in the bales, as I wish these curtains to be made up on a simple, useful pattern, without that paltry trash of drapery, &c &c . . . . The chairs will be most welcome. Packing is a most important article, and I must be indebted to your continued goodness for putting that into proper hands "

The building was sufficiently advanced by the beginning of 1824 to admit of the painting being commenced. I therefore, with ten assistants, repaired to Abbotsford on the 21st of February for that purpose The style of the painting having been often discussed during the progress of the building, I had thereby acquired a perfect understanding of Sir Walter's ideas upon the subject, and, consequently, no specific orders were required on this occasion. Indeed Sir Walter was himself often at Abbotsford during the progress of the work.

The old carved oak fitted up in the entrance-hall, gave a key to the decoration of that apartment Above the wainscoting which surrounds the wall there was plain deal-work to which the ancient armor, warlike instruments, banners, &c were to be fixed. The old portraits, mentioned in Sir Walter's letter to Mr Terry, were not hung in this apartment, there being a sufficient quantity of the more appropriate kind of decoration just detailed. At the east end there were two Gothic niches of the richest description, and large enough to contain figures in full suits of armor These, and another very handsome niche at the other end, were constructed of stucco casts from originals in stone at Melrose Abbey. The ceiling and cornice were also of stucco-work, the former representing massive gothic beams reaching from side to side, intersected in the centre by one principal beam reaching from end to end, and resting upon brackets with shields in front of them, and at the intersections in the centre The fire-place was surrounded by a beautifully carved stone chimney-piece, after the cloister arches at Melrose Abbey. The windows were of stained glass. Of these he says, in a letter to Lord Montague (now Duke of Buccleuch), "As I think heraldry is always better than any other subject, I intend that the upper compartment of each window shall have the shield, supporters, &c. of one of the existing dignitaries of the Clan Scott; and, of course, the Duke's arms and your Lordship's will occupy two such posts of distinction The corresponding two will be Harden's and Thirlestane's, the only families now left who have a right to be regarded as chieftains; and the lower compartments of each window will contain eight shields (without accompaniments), of good gentlemen of the name, of whom I can still muster sixteen bearing separate coats of arms." —(*Life of Scott*, vol v p. 269) To the best of my recollection, some difficulty occurred in carrying out the latter part of Sir Walter's idea in regard to these windows, and the coats of arms of the sixteen gentlemen were ultimately painted on the wall on shields arranged round the entrance-door to the study, appearing to be linked together by a chain, painted also on the wall In directing the painting of this apartment, Sir Walter desired that it should all be done in imitation of oak. not like wood-work newly fitted up, but to resemble the old oak carvings as much as possible Neither would he allow it to appear like old oak newly varnished, as he had strictly forbid the varnishing of the old oak itself. He said, if it were possible, he should like the whole to appear somewhat weather-beaten and faded, as if it had stood untouched for many years The doors, architraves, and part of the wainscoting were fitted up with new oak, and this he also ordered to be toned down to match the old carvings. All this was accomplished to his entire satisfaction.

The shields on the ceiling, amounting to about fifty or sixty in number, and about a foot and a half square, were, like the rest of the ceiling-work, made of stucco, and quite plain. Those that covered the intersections of the beams along the centre he allotted to the armorial bearings of his own family. Sir Walter took great interest in this part of the decorations. And in writing to Mr. Terry on the 29th October, 1843, he says, "The interior of the hall is finished with scutcheons, sixteen of which running along the centre, I intend to paint with my own quarterings, so far as I know them, for I am uncertain as yet of two on my mother's side. . . . The scutcheons on the cornice I propose to charge with the blazonry of all the Border clans, eighteen in number, and so many of the great families, not clans, as will occupy the others. The windows are to be painted with the different bearings of different families of the clan of Scott, which with their quarterings and impalings will make a pretty display."—(*Ibid.* v. p. 313) Again, in writing to Mr. Constable on the 29th of March, 1824, he says,—"For the roof-tree I tried to blazon my own quarterings, and succeed easily with eight on my father's side ; but on my mother's side I stuck fast at the mother of my great-great-grandfather . . If I could find out these Rutherfords, and who they married, I could complete my tree, which is otherwise correct; but if not, I will paint clouds on these three shields, with the motto *Vixerunt portes ante* "—(*Ibid.* v. p. 345.) Sir Walter did not succeed in his inquiries, therefore the three shields in question were painted in clouds, but with a different motto from the above, the words of which I do not recollect The shields at the ends of the cross-beams contained the scutcheons of the eighteen Border clans, and those of about twenty other distinguished families. For some of these Sir Walter had got small sketches by a young gentleman of Jedburgh, an amateur, but they were far from being correct, which, when pointed out to Sir Walter, he said it would be better to begin *de novo*, and take them all, or as many as I could find, from Nisbet's heraldry and other books in his study, and added, that I might come into that apartment for this purpose at all times, whether he was there or not, as it would not in the least disturb him. One error committed in the drawings of the amateur amused him a good deal. Amongst the sub-ordinaries in heraldry there is a figure called Torteaux, representing a little circular cake of bread, of which Nisbet quotes from a Spanish herald the following story —"One of the kings of Spain being to give battle to the Moors, convened his principal captains and commanders to eat, telling them, that so many cakes as they did eat, each of them would kill as many Moors and after a memorable victory, considering how many cakes each had ate, some five, eight, or twelve, took as many torteauxes in their arms, or added them to their ancient bearings, and this is the reason why so many torteauxes are carried in the arms of the nobles of Andalusia, so that they are taken by the French, Italians, Spanish, English, and us, for cakes of bread" Sir Walter seemed much interested by this quotation, and as the amateur had emblazoned the shield of the Blairs of Balthyock with three tortoises, instead of torteauxes, he was greatly pleased that the error had been detected, for he considered, as he expresses himself on a similar subject, in the letter to Mr Constable already referred to—"These things are trifles when correct, but very absurd and contemptible when otherwise." He was much amused with the idea of the ancestor of the Blairs having eaten three reptiles instead of cakes, before going to battle, and often afterwards referred to this particular shield, and the story of the Spanish king.

When all the shields were emblazoned, Sir Walter gave me instructions to paint an inscription in ancient black letters along the top of the wall on the side opposite the entrance door, the inscription was nearly in the following words. "These be the coats armories of the clans and men of name wha keepit the Scottish Borders in the days of old" This was so arranged that one long word, or two short ones, came between each pair of shields, and when finished greatly improved the general effect in a decorative point of view, by forming a connecting link between the scutcheons on that side of the hall. On observing to Sir Walter that something of a similar kind would be required to balance it on the other side, he agreed that there certainly was a want of balance, and said he would bring me something to fill up the vacant spaces In a very few minutes he returned with the following context, written on a slip of paper—"They were worthy and brave in their times, and in their defence God he them defended"

Before hanging up the armor, or placing the full suits of mail in the niches, Sir Walter was most anxious to have all the steel and iron secured from rusting, which he feared it would be liable to in an apartment like the entrance-hall where the external air was necessarily so often admitted, and in all states of the atmosphere too This I accomplished by having all the coats of mail and warlike instruments cleaned with rotton-stone and water, and, when perfectly dry, placing them before a good fire, and giving them a thin coat of the clearest copal varnish. I saw them about fifteen years thereafter without the slightest mark of rust upon them, and I believe they remain so till this day While the cleaning and varnishing was going on, Sir Walter carefully watched its progress, and used often to admire the effects of the light, as it fell upon the armor through the stained glass windows while it lay in groups upon the floor of the hall.

On one occasion when a largeish quantity of it was heaped up opposite the windows, and by chance pretty well grouped, the sun's rays striking upon it tinged with the various hues of the stained glass, he expressed himself strongly regarding its beauty, adding, "I wish my friend William Allan were here—what a glorious study for him!" In regard to the armor, he says to Mr. Terry, in writing to him on the 9th of January 1823—"My wainscot will not be altogether seven feet—about six. Higher it cannot be because of the pattern of the Dunfermline part; any lower I would not have it, because the armor, &c. must be suspended beyond the reach of busy rude fingers to which a hall is exposed You understand I mean to keep lighter, smaller, and more ornate objects of curiosity in the present little room, and have only the massive and large specimens, with my fine collection of horns, &c. in the hall"

In reference to the cedar already mentioned, he says in the same letter—"The cedar, I assure you, is quite beautiful. I have seen it sawn out into planks, and every one who looks at it agrees it will be more beautiful than oak. Indeed, what I have seen of it put to that use, bears no comparison unless with such heart of oak as Baldock employed, and that you know is veneered I do not go on the ciy in this, but practical knowledge. Mr Waugh, my neighbor, a West Indian Planter (but himself bred a joiner) has finished the prettiest apartment with it that I ever saw. . . . I give up the Roslin drop in the oratory; indeed I have long seen it would not do. I think the termination of it may be employed as the central part of Mr. Atkinson's beautiful plan for the recess in the library; by the by, the whole of that ceiling, with the heads we have got, will be the prettiest thing ever seen in these parts."—(P 239)

The whole of this ceiling, with its pendants, was painted in imitation of the cedar of which the fittings were made; but the wall between the top of the book-cases and ceiling gave Sir Walter a great deal of concern. This formed a narrow stripe all round the apartment, and it could not be done in any of the usual modes of wall decoration, as the book-cases were actually part of the fittings of the room, and had not the slightest appearance of being placed against the wall like pieces of furniture. At last the idea of a piece of painted imitation drapery hanging from the cornice was suggested to him, and he at once adopted it. It was painted of a sombre hue of green, in order to relieve the red hue of the cedar, which it effectually did, and that it might also partake of the richness of the backs of the books with which the cases underneath it were filled, it was embellished with devices in gold color. Sir Walter often said that this was the only part of the decorative painting that he could not come to a decision upon in his own mind, but when he saw it finished he expressed himself highly gratified, and his mind relieved of an uncertainty that had occasioned him some uneasiness

Notwithstanding the length of this note, it can scarcely be considered complete without the addition of the following quotation from the correspondence of the great man whose ideas on decoration it is intended to elucidate. To his friend Mr. Terry he says, on 18th February, 1824,—"Your very kind letter reached me here (Abbotsford) so that I was enabled to send you immediately an accurate sketch of the windows and chimney-sides of the drawing-room, to measurement. I should like the mirrors handsome, and the frames plain, the color of the hangings (meaning the paper) is green, with rich Chinese figures On the side of the window I intend to have exactly beneath the glass, a plain white side-table of the purest marble, on which to place Chantrey's bust A truncated pillar of the same marble will be its support; and I think that, besides the mirror above, there will be a plate of mirror below the table; these memoranda will enable Baldock [a London upholsterer] to say at what price these points can be handsomely accomplished. I have not yet spoken about the marble table; perhaps they may be all got in London I shall be willing to give a handsome, but not an extravagant price I am much obliged to Mr. Baldock for his confidence about the screen. But what says poor Richard? 'Those who want money when they come to buy, are apt to want money when they come to pay.' Again poor Dick observes,—

> 'That in many you find the true gentleman's fate,
> Ere his house is complete he has sold his estate.'—

So we will adjourn the consideration of the screen till other times; let us first have the needful got and paid for. The stuff for the windows in the drawing-room is the crimson damask silk we bought last year. I inclose a scrap of it that the fringe may be made to match. I propose they should be hung with large handsome brass rings upon a brass cylinder, and I believe it would be best to have these articles from London,—I mean the rings and cylinders; but I dislike much complication in the mode of drawing them separate, as it is eternally going wrong; those which divide in the middle, drawing back on each side like the curtain of an old-fashioned bed, and when drawn back are secured by a loop and tassel, are, I think, the handsomest, and can easily be made on the spot; the fringe should be silk, of course. I think the curtains of the library, considering the purpose of the room, require no fringe at all. We have, I believe, settled that they shall not be drawn in a line across the recess, as in the drawing-room, but shall circle along the inside of the windows. I refer myself to Mr. Atkinson about the fringe, but I think a little mixture of gold would look handsome with the crimson silk. As for the library, a yellow fringe, if any. I send a draught of the window inclosed; the architraves are not yet up in the library, but they are accurately computed from the drawings of my friend Mr. Atkinson. There is plenty of time to think about these matters, for of course the rooms must be painted before they are put up. I saw the presses yesterday; they are very handsome, and remind me of the awful job of arranging my books About July, Abbotsford, I think, will be finished, when I shall, like the old Duke of Queensberry who built Drumlanrig, fold up the accounts in a sealed parcel, with a label bidding 'the deil pike out the een of ony of my successors that shall open it.'"

Note D, p 156

Upon this subject Professor Hosking makes the following excellent remarks—"The exhumated city of Pompeii has very clearly proved that notwithstanding the extent and general beauty of the public buildings of the Romans, the houses of the commonalty were exceedingly plain and confined, while those of the higher classes, though internally elegant, were externally unpretending The rooms were small and badly arranged, imperfectly secluded from the public gaze, and quite exposed to the inmates; pervious alike to the summer's heat and winter's cold. Indeed the house of a Roman gentleman presents a very convenient model for a prison, but without many of the comforts which in modern times are thought necessary even in such places.

"In consequence of the refinements which now pervade the manners, habits, and customs of civilized life, and civilization having extended itself from the noble and the learned through almost the whole social system, men are no longer contented to admire the beauty and magnificence of public edifices, whether ecclesiastical or civil, and to witness the splendor and elegance of the palaces and mansions of the wealthy; but all are anxious to see in their own habitations that degree of decoration and beauty which they find so productive of pleasure and pleasurable emotions Thus architecture is no longer confined to the temples of the Divinity and the palaces of the great, but its beauties are sought everywhere. In every edifice whose inhabitants have been fitted by education and habit to appreciate and enjoy the charm which arises from symmetry of form, beauty of proportion, and elegance of detail, the aid of architecture is required."—(*Encyclopædia Britannica*, Art '*Architecture*,' p. 28) In another part (p 44) the Professor observes, that "A person accustomed to the comforts and conveniences of houses in this country finds much to complain of in a modern Italian mansion, but not so much as an Italian would in the house of an ancient Roman; and from analogy we may believe that a Roman of the empire would have reason to complain of a Grecian domicile, even of the Periclean age; and a Greek again might have been abridged of the comforts of his house in the palace of an Egyptian "

PRACTICAL

AND

SCIENTIFIC BOOKS,

PUBLISHED BY

HENRY CAREY BAIRD,

INDUSTRIAL PUBLISHER,

No. 406 WALNUT STREET,

PHILADELPHIA.

☞ Any of the following Books will be sent by mail, free of postage, at the publication price. Catalogues furnished on application.

American Miller and Millwright's Assistant:

A new and thoroughly revised Edition, with additional Engravings. By William Carter Hughes. In one Volume, 12mo. $1.50

Armengaud, Amoroux, and Johnson.

THE PRACTICAL DRAUGHTSMAN'S BOOK OF INDUSTRIAL DESIGN, and Machinist's and Engineer's Drawing Companion; forming a complete course of Mechanical Engineering and Architectural Drawing. From the French of M. Armengaud the elder, Prof. of Design in the Conservatoire of Arts and Industry, Paris, and MM. Armengaud the younger, and Amoroux, Civil Engineers. Rewritten and arranged with additional matter and plates, selections from and examples of the most useful and generally employed mechanism of the day. By William Johnson, Assoc. Inst C. E., Editor of "The Practical Mechanic's Journal" Illustrated by fifty folio steel plates and fifty wood-cuts. A new edition. 4to.....................$10.00

Among the contents are:—*Linear Drawing, Definitions and Problems,* Plate I Applications, Designs for inlaid Pavements, Ceilings, and Balconies, Plate II Sweeps, Sections, and Mouldings, Plate III. Elementary

Gothic Forms and Rosettes, Plate IV. Ovals, Ellipses, Parabolas, and Volutes, Plate V. Rules and Practical Data *Study of Projections*, Elementary Principles, Plate VI. Of Prisms and other Solids, Plate VII Rules and Practical Data. *On Coloring Sections, with Applications*—Conventional Colors, Composition or Mixture of Colors, Plate X *Continuation of the Study of Projections*—Use of sections—details of machinery, Plate XI Simple applications—spindles, shafts, couplings, wooden patterns, Plate XII Method of constructing a wooden model or pattern of a coupling, Elementary applications—rails and chairs for railways, Plate XIII. *Rules and Practical Data*—Strength of material, Resistance to compression or crushing force, Tensional Resistance, Resistance to flexure. Resistance to torsion Friction of surfaces in contact.

THE INTERSECTION AND DEVELOPMENT OF SURFACES WITH APPLICATIONS.—*The Intersection of Cylinders and Cones*, Plate XIV *The Delineation and Development of Helices, Screws, and Serpentines*, Plate XV. Application of the helix—the construction of a staircase, Plate XVI The Intersection of surfaces—applications to stopcocks, Plate XVII *Rules and Practical Data*—Steam, Unity of heat, Heating surface, Calculation of the dimensions of boilers, Dimensions of fire grates, Chimneys, Safety valves.

THE STUDY AND CONSTRUCTION OF TOOTHED GEAR—Involute, cycloid, and epicycloid, Plates XVIII and XIX. Involute, Fig 1, Plate XVIII. Cycloid, Fig 2, Plate XVIII. External epicycloid, described by a circle rolling about a fixed circle inside it, Fig. 3, Plate XIX Internal epicycloid, Fig 2, Plate XIX. Delineation of a rack and pinion in gear, Fig. 4, Plate XVIII Gearing of a worm with a worm-wheel, Figs. 5 and 6, Plate XVIII. *Cylindrical or Spur Gearing*, Plate XIX. Practical delineation of a couple of Spur-wheels, Plate XX. *The Delineation and Construction of Wooden Patterns for Toothed Wheels*, Plate XXI. *Rules and Practical Data*—Toothed gearing, Angular and circumferential velocity of wheels, Dimensions of gearing, Thickness of the teeth, Pitch of the teeth, Dimensions of the web, Number and dimensions of the arms, wooden patterns

CONTINUATION OF THE STUDY OF TOOTHED GEAR.—Design for a pair of bevel-wheels in gear, Plate XXII. Construction of wooden patterns for a pair of bevel-wheels, Plate XXIII *Involute and Helical Teeth*, Plate XXIV *Contrivances for obtaining Differential Movements*—The delineation of eccentrics and cams, Plate XXV *Rules and Practical Data*—Mechanical work of effect, The simple machines, Centre of gravity, On estimating the power of prime movers, Calculation for the brake, The fall of bodies, Momentum, Central forces

ELEMENTARY PRINCIPLES OF SHADOWS—*Shadows of Prisms, Pyramids and Cylinders*, Plate XXVI *Principles of Shading*, Plate XXVII *Continuation of the Study of Shadows*, Plate XXVIII. *Tuscan Order*, Plate XXIX. *Rules and Practical Data*—Pumps, Hydrostatic principles, Forcing pumps, Lifting and forcing pumps, The Hydrostatic press, Hydrostatical calculations and data—discharge of water through different orifices, Gauging of a water-course of uniform section and fall, Velocity of the bottom of water-courses, Calculations of the discharge of water through rectangular orifices of narrow edges, Calculation of the discharge of water through overshot outlets, To determine the width of an overshot outlet, To determine the depth of the outlet, Outlet with a spout or duct

APPLICATION OF SHADOWS TO TOOTHED GEAR, Plate XXX. *Application of Shadows to Screws*, Plate XXXI. *Application of Shadows to a Boiler and its Furnace*, Plate XXXII *Shading in Black—Shading in Colors*, Plate XXXIII.

THE CUTTING AND SHAPING OF MASONRY, Plate XXXIV. *Rules and Practical Data*—Hydraulic motors, Undershot water-wheels, with plane floats and a circular channel, Width, Diameter, Velocity, Number, and capacity of the buckets Useful effect of the water-wheel, Overshot water-wheels, Water-wheels with radical floats, Water-wheel with curved buckets, Turbines. *Remarks on Machine Tools.*

THE STUDY OF MACHINERY AND SKETCHING—Various applications and combinations: *The Sketching of Machinery*, Plates XXXV and XXXVI. *Drilling Machines; Motive Machines;* Water-wheels, Construction and setting up of water-wheels, Delineation of water-wheels, Design of a water-wheel Sketch of a water-wheel, *Overshot Water-wheels, Water Pumps*, Plate XXXVII. *Steam Motors*, High-pressure expansive steam engine, Plates XXXVIII., XXXIX., and XL. *Details of Construction, Movements of the Distribution and Expansion Valves, Rules and Practical Data*—Steam-engines: Low-pressure condensing engines without expansion valve, Diameter of piston, Velocities, Steam pipes and passages, Air-pump and condenser, Cold-water and feed-pumps, High-pressure expansive engines, Medium pressure condensing and expansive steam-engine, Conical pendulum or centrifugal governor

OBLIQUE PROJECTIONS.—Application of rules to the delineation of an oscillating cylinder, Plate XLI

PARALLEL PERSPECTIVE.—Principles and applications, Plate XLII

TRUE PERSPECTIVE.—Elementary principles, Plate XLIII Applications—flour mill driven by belts, Plates XLIV. and XLV. Description of the mill, Representation of the mill in perspective, Notes of recent improvements in flour mills, Schiele's mill, Mullin's "ring millstone," Barnett's millstone, Hastie's arrangement for driving mills, Currie's improvements in millstones. *Rules and Practical Data*—Work performed by various machines, Flour mills, Saw-mills, Veneer sawing machines, Circular saws.

EXAMPLES OF FINISHED DRAWINGS OF MACHINERY.—Plate A, Balance water-meter; Plate B, Engineer's shaping machine; Plates C, D, E, Express locomotive engine; Plate F, Wood planing machine; Plate G, Washing machine for piece goods, Plate H, power-loom; Plate I, Duplex steam boiler; Plate J, Direct-acting marine engines

DRAWING INSTRUMENTS.

Arrowsmith. Paper-Hanger's Companion:

By James Arrowsmith. 12mo., cloth................$1.25

Baird. The American Cotton Spinner, and Manager's and Carder's Guide:

A Practical Treatise on Cotton Spinning; giving the Dimensions and Speed of Machinery, Draught and Twist Calculations, etc ; with notices of recent Improvements · together with Rules and Examples for making changes in the sizes and numbers of Roving and Yarn. Compiled from the papers of the late Robert H. Baird. 12mo $1 50

CONTENTS.—Introduction; On the Plan of a Factory Building, On the Main Gearing; On Water-wheels; Calculations of Horse-Power for Propelling Cotton Spinning Machinery; Willie or Picking Machine, On Willeying Cotton; Spreading Machine; On Spreading Cotton; Carding; Cards and Carding; Covering Emery Rollers and Emeries; The Drawing-frame, Roving; General Remarks on Drawing and Roving; Throstles; Remarks on Throstles, Mule Spinning, General Observations on Mule Spinning; Weaving, Belting; Miscellaneous matters.

Beans. A Treatise on Railroad Curves and the Location of Railroads:

By E. W. Beans, C. E. 12mo. (In press.)

Bishop. A History of American Manufactures:

From 1608 to 1866: exhibiting the Origin and Growth of the Principal Mechanic Arts and Manufactures, from the Earliest Colonial Period to the Present Time; with a Notice of the Important Inventions, Tariffs, and the Results of each Decennial Census. By J. Leander Bishop, M. D ; to which is added Notes on the Principal Manufacturing Centres and Remarkable Manufactories. By Edward Young and Edwin T. Freedley. In three vols., 8vo.....................$8.00

Blinn. A Practical Workshop Companion for Tin, Sheet-Iron, and Copper-Plate Workers:

Containing Rules for describing various kinds of Patterns used by Tin, Sheet-Iron, and Copper-Plate Workers; Practical Geometry; Mensuration of Surfaces and Solids; Tables of the Weights of Metals, Lead Pipe, etc ; Tables of Areas and Circumferences of Circles; Japan, Varnishes, Lackers, Cements, Compositions, etc., etc. By Leroy J. Blinn, Master Mechanic. With over One Hundred Illustrations. 12mo. $2.50

CONTENTS.—*Rules for Describing Patterns*.—An Envelope for a Cone, A Frustrum of a Cone, A Can top or Deck flange; A Pattern for, or an Envelope for a Frustrum of a Cone, A Tapering Oval Article to be in four Sections, A Tapering Oval Article to be in two Sections, A Tapering Oval Article, A Tapering Oval and Oblong Article, the sides to be Straight, with Quarter Circle corners, to be in two Sections, A Tapering Oval or Oblong Article, the sides to be Straight, one end to be a Semicircle, the other end to be Straight, with Quarter Circle corners, to be in two Sections, A Tapering Oval or Oblong Article, the sides to be Straight, with Semicircle ends, to be in two Sections, Covering of Circular Roofs, Two different Principles, To cover a Dome by the first Method, To cover a Dome by the second Method, To ascertain the Outline of a Course of covering to a Dome, without reference to a Section of the Dome, To describe a Pattern for a Tapering Square Article, A Square Tapering Article to be in two Sections, A Tapering Article, the Base to be Square, and the Top a Circle, in two Sections, A Tapering Article, the Base to be a Rectangle, and the Top Square, in two Sections, A Tapering Article, the Base to be a Rectangle, and the Top a Circle, in two Sections, A Tapering Article, the Top and Base to be a Rectangle, in two Sections, Tapering Octagon Top or Cover, A Miter Joint at Right Angles for a Semicircle Gutter, A Miter Joint at any Angle for a Semicircle Gutter, A Miter Joint for an O G Gutter at Right Angles, A Miter Joint for an O G Cornice at Right Angles, also an Offset, An Octagon O G Lamp Top or Cover, A T Pipe at Right Angles, A T Pipe at any Angle, A T Pipe, the Collar to be smaller than the Main Pipe, A T Pipe at any Angle, the Collar to set on one side of the Main Pipe, A Pipe to fit a flat Surface at any Angle, as the Side of a Roof of a Building, A Pipe to fit two flat Surfaces, as the Roof of a Building, An Elbow at Right Angles, An Elbow Pattern at any Angle, An Elbow in three Sections, An Elbow in four Sections, An Elbow in five Sections, A Tapering Elbow, An Oval Boiler Cover, A Flange for a Pipe that goes on the Roof of a Building, Octagon or Square Top or Cover, Steamer Cover, An Ellipse or Oval, having two Diameters given, An Ellipse with the Rule and Compasses, the Transverse and Conjugate Diameters being given, that is, the Length and Width, To find the Centre and the two Arcs of an Ellipse, To find the Radius and Versed Sine for a given Frustrum of a Cone, Practical Geometry, Decimal Equivalents to Fractional Parts of Lineal Measurement, Definitions of Arithmetical Signs, Mensuration of Surfaces, Mensuration of Solids and Capacities of Bodies, Tables of Weights of Iron, Copper, and Lead, Tables of the Circumferences and Areas of Circles, Sizes and capacity of Tinware in form of Frustrum of a Cone, such as Pans, Dish Kettles, Pails, Coffee-pots, Wash Bowls, Dippers, Measures, Druggists' and Liquor Dealers' Measures, American Lap Welded Iron Boiler Flues, Table of Effects upon Bodies by Heat, Weight of Water, Effects produced by Water in an Aeriform State, Practical Properties of Water, Effects produced by Water in its Natural State, Effects of Heat at certain Temperatures, Tempering, Effects produced by Air in its Natural and in a Rarefied State, Table of the Expansion of Atmospheric Air by Heat, Size, Length, Breadth, and Weight of Tin Plates, Crystallized Tin Plate, List of Calibre and Weights of Lead Pipe, Calibre and Weights of Fountain or Aqueduct Pipes, To ascertain the Weights of Pipes of various Metals, and any Diameter required, Weight of a Square Foot of Sheet Iron, Copper, and Brass, as per Birmingham Wire Gauge, Recapitulation of

Weights of Various Substances *Practical Receipts.*—Japanning and Varnishing, Varnishes—Miscellaneous, Lackers, Cements, Miscellaneous Receipts, Britannia, Solders, etc., Strength of Materials.

Booth and Morfit. The Encyclopedia of Chemistry, Practical and Theoretical:

Embracing its application to the Arts, Metallurgy, Mineralogy, Geology, Medicine, and Pharmacy. By James C. Booth, Melter and Refiner in the United States Mint, Professor of Applied Chemistry in the Franklin Institute, etc., assisted by Campbell Morfit, author of "Chemical Manipulations," etc. 7th edition. Complete in one volume, royal 8vo. 978 pages, with numerous wood-cuts and other illustrations $5.00

Brewer; (The Complete Practical.)

Or Plain, Concise, and Accurate Instructions in the Art of Brewing Beer, Ale, Porter, etc., etc., and the Process of making all the Small Beers. By M. Lafayette Byrn, M D. With Illustrations. 12mo $1.25

Buckmaster. The Elements of Mechanical Physics.

By J. C Buckmaster, late Student in the Goverment School of Mines; Certified Teacher of Science by the Department of Science and Art; Examiner in Chemistry and Physics in the Royal College of Preceptors, and late Lecturer in Chemistry and Physics of the Royal Polytechnic Institute. Illustrated with numerous engravings. In one volume, 12mo. $2.00

CONTENTS —*The Elements of Mechanical Physics*—CHAP. I —Statics and Dynamics; Force; Gravitation and Weight; On Matter—its Mass, Density, and Volume II —Centre of Gravity; Stable and Unstable Equilibrium, To find the Centre of Gravity of a Material Straight Line of Uniform Density; To find the Centre of Gravity of two heavy Points joined by a rigid bar without Weight; To find the Centre of Gravity of a number of heavy points, To find the Centre of Gravity of a Material Plain Triangle III —Levers; Levers are of three kinds; Virtual Velocity; Balances; The Safety Valve; Mechanical Combinations and their Advantages IV —The Wheel and Axle; The Compound Wheel and Axle. V —The Pulley, Wheels and Pinions; Cranks and Fly-Wheel VI —The Inclined Plane, The Wedge; The Screw VII —Composition and Resolution of Forces. VIII.—Falling Bodies; Ascent of Bodies; Projection of Bodies Horizontally. IX.—Momentum X —Sound; The Pendulum.

Elements of Hydrostatics —CHAP I —Hydrostatics; Bramah Hydrostatic Press II —Specific Gravity; Table of Specific Gravities III —Elastic Fluids; The Air Pump and its Operation, The Construction of the Condenser and its Operation; The Barometer; The Action of the Siphon; How to Graduate a common Thermometer, To Reduce the Degrees of a Thermometer in Fahrenheit's scale to a centigrade and the converse; The Construction of a Siphon gauge; The Construction of a common Pump and its Operation; The Construction and Operation of a Force Pump; The Operation of a Fire Engine; The Operation of a Lifting Pump, The Hydraulic Ram, The Archimedian Screw; The Chain Pump; Mercurial Steam Gauge; Examination Papers.

APPENDIX.—Examples; Answers to Examples.

Bullock. The Rudiments of Architecture and Building:

For the use of Architects, Builders, Draughtsmen, Machinists, Engineers and Mechanics. Edited by John Bullock, author of "The American Cottage Builder" Illustrated by Two Hundred and Fifty Engravings. In one volume, 8vo.......................................$3.50

Burgh. The Slide Valve Practically Considered.

By N. P. Burgh, Engineer. Completely Illus. 12mo...$2.00

Burgh. Practical Rules for the Proportion of Modern Engines and Boilers for Land and Marine Purposes.

By N. P. Burgh, Engineer. 12mo...................$2.00

CONTENTS — High Pressure Engines; Beam Engines (condensing); Marine Screw Engines; Oscillating Engines; Valves, etc ; Land and Marine Boilers *Miscellaneous* —Coal Bunkers, Marine; Decimals, etc ; Eccentric, Position of, for Land Engines, Eccentric, Position of for Marine Screw Engines, Fire Bars, Keys and Cotters, Link for Land Engine, Radius of Levers, Link for Oscillating Engine, Radius of, Link for Marine Screw Engine, Radius of; Proportion of Connecting Rods having Strap Ends, Paddle Wheels, Centres of Radius Rods, Plummer Blocks; Proportions of Steam Cocks with Plugs secured by Nuts and Screws; Proportion of Marine Cocks; Proportions of Bolts, Nuts, etc ; Proportions of Pins, Studs, Flanges etc.; Proportions of Copper Pipes, Proportions of Engines; Sliding Quadrant; Toothed Wheels (Gearing). *Proportions of Engines Produced by the Rules* Proportions of an Engine 20 HP nominal, Proportions of a Condensing Beam Engine 150 HP nominal; Proportions of a Pair of Marine Engines of 200 HP Collectively, Proportions of a Pair of Oscillating Engines of 400 HP Collectively, Proportions of Boilers.

Byrne. Pocket Book for Railroad and Civil Engineers.

Containing New, Exact, and Concise Methods for Laying out Railroad Curves, Switches, Frog Angles and Crossings; the Staking out of Work; Leveling; the Calculation of Cuttings, Embankments, Earth-work, etc. By Oliver Byrne. Illustrated, 18mo $1 25

Byrne. The Practical Metal-Worker's Assistant.

Comprising Metallurgic Chemistry; the Arts of Working all Metals and Alloys, Forging of Iron and Steel; Hardening and Tempering; Melting and Mixing; Casting and Founding; Works in Sheet Metal; the Process dependent on the Ductility of the Metals, Soldering; and the most Improved Processes and Tools employed by Metal-Workers. With the Application of the Art of Electro-Metallurgy to Manufacturing Processes; collected from Original Sources, and from the Works of Holtzapffel, Bergeron, Leupold, Plumier, Napier, and others. By Oliver Byrne A New, Revised, and Improved Edition, with additions by John Scoffern, M. B., William Clay, William Fairbairn, F. R. S., and James Napier. With Five Hundred and Ninety-two Engravings, illustrating every Branch of the Subject. In one volume, 8vo. 652 pages $7.00

CONTENTS —On Metallurgic Chemistry; Special Metallurgic Operations; Recently Patented Refining Processes; Refining and Working of Iron; Manufacture of Steel; Forging Iron and Steel; On Wrought-Iron in Large Masses; General Examples of Welding, Hardening and Tempering, Hardening Cast and Wrought-Iron, On the Application of Iron to Ship-Building; The Metals and Alloys most commonly used; Remarks on the Character of the Metals and Alloys; Melting and Mixing the Metals; Casting and Founding, Works in Sheet Metal made by Joining; Works in Sheet Metal made by raising and flattening of thin Plates of Metal; Processes dependent on Ductility, Soldering, Shears, Punches, Drills; Screw-cutting Tools, Electro-Metallurgy.

Byrne. The Handbook for the Artisan, Mechanic, and Engineer.

By Oliver Byrne. Illustrated by 11 large plates and 185 wood engravings. 8vo.............................. $5 00

CONTENTS —Grinding Cutting Tools on the Ordinary Grindstone; Sharpening Cutting Tools on the Oilstone; Setting Razors; Sharpening Cutting Tools with Artificial Grinders, Production of Plane Surfaces by Abrasion: Production of Cylindrical Surfaces by Abrasion, Production of Conical Surfaces by Abrasion, Production of Spherical Surfaces by Abrasion, Glass Cutting; Lapidary Work; Setting, Cutting, and Polishing Flat and Rounded Works, Cutting Faucets; Lapidary Apparatus for Amateurs; Gem and Glass Engraving; Seal and Gem Engraving; Cameo Cutting; Glass Engraving, Varnishing. and Lackering, General Remarks upon Abrasive Processes; Dictionary of Apparatus; Materials and Processes for Grinding and Polishing, commonly employed in the Mechanical and Useful Arts.

Byrne. The Practical Model Calculator:

For the Engineer, Mechanic, Manufacturer of Engine Work, Naval Architect, Miner, and Millwright. By Oliver Byrne. 1 vol. 8vo, nearly 600 pages $4 50

The principal objects of this work are to establish model calculations to guide practical men and students, to illustrate every practical rule and principle by numerical calculations, systematically arranged; to give information and data indispensable to those for whom it is intended, thus surpassing in value any other book of its character; to economize the labor of the practical man, and to render his every-day calculations easy and comprehensive. It will be found to be one of the most complete and valuable practical books ever published.

Cabinet-maker's and Upholsterer's Companion.

Comprising the Rudiments and Principles of Cabinet-making and Upholstery, with Familiar Instructions, illustrated by Examples for attaining a proficiency in the Art of Drawing, as applicable to Cabinet-work; the processes of Veneering, Inlaying, and Buhl-work; the Art of Dyeing and Staining Wood Bone, Tortoise Shell, etc. Directions for Lackering

Japanning, and Varnishing; to make French Polish, to prepare the best Glues, Cements and Compositions, and a number of Receipts particularly useful for workmen generally. By J. Stokes. In one vol., 12mo. With Illustrations...$1.25

Calvert. On Improvements and Progress in Dyeing and Calico Printing since 1851.

Illustrated with Numerous Specimens of Printed and Dyed Fabrics. By Dr. F. Grace Calvert, F. R. S., F. C. S. A Lecture delivered before the Society of Arts. Revised and enlarged by the author. (*Nearly Ready*)

Carey. The Works of Henry C. Carey:

CONTRACTION OR EXPANSION? REPUDIATION OR RESUMPTION? Letters to Hon. Hugh McCulloch. 8vo...38

FINANCIAL CRISES, their Causes and Effects 8vo paper...25

FRENCH AND AMERICAN TARIFFS: Compared in a Series of Letters addressed to Mons. M. Chevalier. 8vo. paper...50

HARMONY OF INTERESTS: Agricultural, Manufacturing, and Commercial. 8vo., paper.......................$1.00
Do. do. cloth.......................1.50

LETTERS TO THE PRESIDENT OF THE UNITED STATES. Paper...75

MANUAL OF SOCIAL SCIENCE. Condensed from Carey's "Principles of Social Science." By Kate McKean 1 vol., 12mo.................................$2 25

The Text-Book of the Universities of Berlin (Prussia), Pennsylvania, and Michigan, and of the College of New Jersey, Princeton.

MISCELLANEOUS WORKS: comprising "Harmony of Interests," "Money," "Letters to the President," "French and American Tariffs," "Financial Crises," "The Way to Outdo England without Fighting Her," "Resources of the Union," "The Public Debt," "Contraction or Expansion?" etc, etc. 1 vol. 8vo., cloth........................$3.50

MONEY: A LECTURE before the N. Y. Geographical and Statistical Society. 8vo., paper.......................25

PAST, PRESENT, AND FUTURE 8vo...........$2.50

PRINCIPLES OF SOCIAL SCIENCE. 3 volumes. 8vo., cloth...$10.00

CONTENTS — Volume I: Of Science and its Methods; Of Man, the Subject of Social Science; Of Increase in the Numbers of Mankind; Of the Occupation of the Earth; Of Value; Of Wealth; Of the Formation of Society;

Of Appropriation; Of Changes of Matter in Place; Of Mechanical and Chemical Changes in the Forms of Matter. Volume II: Of Vital Changes in the Form of Matter, Of the Instrument of Association. Volume III: Of Production and Consumption, Of Accumulation, Of Circulation, Of Distribution, Of Concentration and Centralization; Of Competition; Of Population; Of Food and Population, Of Colonization; Of the Malthusian Theory; Of Commerce; Of the Societary Organization; Of Social Science.

THE PUBLIC DEBT, LOCAL AND NATIONAL. How to provide for its discharge while lessening the burden of Taxation Letter to David A Wells, Esq, U. S Revenue Commission. 8vo., paper 25

THE RESOURCES OF THE UNION. A Lecture read, Dec 1865, before the American Geographical and Statistical Society, N. Y, and before the American Association for the Advancement of Social Science, Boston 25

THE SLAVE-TRADE, DOMESTIC AND FOREIGN: Why it Exists, and How it may be Extinguished. 12mo. cloth $1 50

THE WAY TO OUTDO ENGLAND WITHOUT FIGHTING HER LETTERS TO THE HON. SCHUYLER COLFAX, Speaker of the House of Representatives United States, on "The Paper Question," "The Farmer's Question," "The Iron Question," "The Railroad Question," and the "Currency Question" 8vo., paper 75

Campin. A Practical Treatise on Mechanical Engineering:

Comprising Metallurgy, Moulding, Casting, Forging, Tools, Workshop Machinery, Mechanical Manipulation, Manufacture of Steam-engines, etc, etc With an Appendix on the Analysis of Iron and Iron Ores. By Francis Campin. C. E. To which are added, Observations on the Construction of Steam Boilers and remarks upon Furnaces used for Smoke Prevention; with a Chapter on Explosions By R. Armstrong, C. E., and John Bourne Rules for Calculating the Change Wheels for Screws on a Turning Lathe, and for a Wheel-cutting Machine. By J. La Nicca. Management of Steel, including Forging, Hardening, Tempering, Annealing, Shrinking, and Expansion. And the Case-hardening of Iron. By G Ede. 8vo. Illustrated with 29 plates and 100 wood engravings $6 00

CONTENTS—Introduction—On Metallurgy, On Forging Iron. On Moulding and Casting On Cutting Tools, On Workshop Machinery, On Manipulation, On the Physical Basis of the Steam-engine; On the Principles of Mechanical Construction, On the General Arrangement of the Steam-engine, On the General Principles of Steam Boilers, Preliminary considerations on the Applicability of various kinds of Steam-engines to various purposes, On the details of Steam-engines; On Pumps and Valves, On Steam Boilers; On Propellers; On various applications of Steam-power and Apparatus connected therewith; On Pumping Engines, On Rotative Engines; On Marine Engines, On Locomotive Engines, On Road Locomotives, On Steam Fire Engines, On Boilers generally, and a Radical Reform in those for Marine purposes suggested, Smoke Prevention and its fallacies; Remarks on Smoke-burning, by John Bourne, Explosions: an investigation into some of the causes producing them, and into the deterioration of Boilers generally, Rules for Calculating the Change Wheels for Screws on a Turning Lathe, and for a Wheel-cutting Machine, Explanation of the Methods of Calculating Screw Threads, The Management of Steel.

APPENDIX.—The Analysis of Iron and Iron Ores.

GLOSSARY.—INDEX.

Capron de Dole. Dussauce. Blues and Carmines of Indigo.

A Practical Treatise on the Fabrication of every Commercial Product derived from Indigo. By Felicien Capron de Dôle. Translated, with important additions, by Professor H. Dussauce. 12mo....................................$2.50

Clough. The Contractor's Manual and Builder's Price-Book:

Designed to elucidate the method of ascertaining, correctly, the Value and Quantity of every description of Work and Materials, used in the Art of Building, from their Prime Cost in any part of the United States, collected from extensive experience and observation in Building and Designing; to which are added a large variety of Tables, Memoranda, etc., indispensable to all engaged or concerned in erecting buildings of any kind. By A. B. Clough, Architect, 24mo., cloth...75

Colburn. The Locomotive Engine:

Including a Description of its Structure, Rules for Estimating its Capabilities, and Practical Observations on its Construction and Management. By Zerah Colburn. Illustrated. A new edition. 12mo......................$1 25

Daguerreotypist and Photographer's Companion.

12mo., cloth..$1.25

Distiller. (The Complete Practical).

By M. Lafayette Byrn, M. D. With Illust'ns 12mo....$1.50

Duncan. Practical Surveyor's Guide.

By Andrew Duncan. Illustrated. 12mo., cloth......$1 25

Dussauce. Practical Treatise on the Fabrication of Matches, Gun Cotton, and Fulminating Powders.

By Professor H. Dussauce. 12mo...................$3 00

CONTENTS.—*Phosphorus*—History of Phosphorus; Physical Properties; Chemical Properties; Natural State; Preparation of White Phosphorus; Amorphous Phosphorus, and Bonoxide of Lead. *Matches*—Preparation of

Wooden Matches; Matches inflammable by rubbing, without noise, Common Lucifer Matches; Matches without Phosphorus, Candle Matches; Matches with Amorphous Phosphorus, Matches and Rubbers without Phosphorus *Gun Cotton*—Properties; Preparation; Paper Powder; use of Cotton and Paper Powders for Fulminating Primers, etc; Preparation of Fulminating Primers, etc, etc

Dussauce. A New and Complete Treatise on the Arts of Tanning, Currying, and Leather Dressing:

Comprising all the Discoveries and Improvements made in France, Great Britain, and the United States. Edited from Notes and Documents of Messrs. Sallerou, Grouvelle, Duval, Dessables, Labarraque, Payen, René, De Fontenelle, Malapeyre, etc., etc. By Prof. H. Dussauce, Chemist. Illustrated by 212 wood engravings. 8vo................$10 00

Dussauce. Treatise on the Coloring Matters Derived from Coal Tar:

Their Practical Application in Dyeing Cotton, Wool, and Silk; the Principles of the Art of Dyeing and of the Distillation of Coal Tar, with a Description of the most Important New Dyes now in use By Professor H Dussauce, Chemist. 12mo..................................$2.50

Dyer and Color-maker's Companion:

Containing upwards of two hundred Receipts for making Colors, on the most approved principles, for all the various styles and fabrics now in existence; with the Scouring Process, and plain Directions for Preparing, Washing-off, and Finishing the Goods. In one vol., 12mo.............$1 25

Easton. A Practical Treatise on Street or Horse-power Railways:

Their Location, Construction, and Management; with general Plans and Rules for their Organization and Operation; together with Examinations as to their Comparative Advantages over the Omnibus System, and Inquiries as to their Value for Investment; including Copies of Municipal Ordinances relating thereto. By Alexander Easton, C. E Illustrated by 23 plates. 8vo. cloth...................$2 00

Engineer's Handy-Book:

Containing a Series of Useful Calculations for Engineers, Tool-makers, Millwrights, Draughtsmen, Foremen, and Mechanics generally. (*In Press.*)

Erni. Coal Oil and Petroleum:

Their Origin, History, Geology, and Chemistry; with a view of their importance in their bearing on National Industry

By Dr. Henri Erni, Chief Chemist, Department of Agriculture. 12mo.................... ....$2 50

Erni. The Theoretical and Practical Chemistry of Fermentation:

Comprising the Chemistry of Wine, Beer, Distilling of Liquors; with the practical methods of their Chemical examination, preservation, and improvement—such as Gallizing of Wines. With an Appendix, containing well-tested Practical Rules and Receipts for the manufacture, etc., of all kinds of Alcoholic Liquors By Henri Erni, Chief Chemist, Department of Agriculture. (*In Press.*)

Fairbairn. Principles of Mechanism and Machinery of Transmission:

Comprising the Principles of Mechanism, Wheels and Pullies, Strength and Proportions of Shafts, Couplings for Shafts, and Engaging and Disengaging Gear. By Wm. Fairbairn, Esq , C.E., LL D., F.R S., F G.S., Corresponding Member of the National Institute of France, and of the Royal Academy of Turin; Chevalier of the Legion of Honor, etc., etc Illustrated by over 150 wood cuts $2 50

CONTENTS —GENERAL VIEWS, LINK WORK, WRAPPING CONNECTORS, WHEEL-WORK: General Views Relating to Machines; Elementary Forms of Mechanism, Link-work, Wrapping Connectors, Wheel-work producing Motion by rolling Contact; Sliding Pieces producing Motion by sliding Contact, On Wheels and Pullies, Wrapping Connectors; Toothed Wheels, Spur Gearing, Pitch of Wheels, Teeth of Wheels; Bevel Wheels; Skew Bevels, The Worm and Wheel; Strength of the Teeth of Wheels, ON THE STRENGTH AND PROPORTIONS OF SHAFTS, Material of which Shafting is Constructed, Transverse Strain, Torsion, Velocity of Shafts, On Journals, Friction, Lubrication, ON COUPLINGS FOR SHAFTS AND ENGAGING AND DISENGAGING GEAR Couplings, Disengaging and Re-engaging Gear, Hangers, Plumber Blocks, etc, for carrying Shafting, Main Shafts.

Fairbairn. Useful Information for Engineers.

By William Fairbairn. (*In Press*)

Kobell. Erni. Mineralogy Simplified:

A short method of Determining and Classifying Minerals, by means of simple Chemical Experiments in the Wet Way. Translated from the last German edition of F. Von Kobell, with additions, by Henri Erni, M D, Chief Chemist, Departpartment of Agriculture, author of "Coal Oil and Petroleum" In one volume, 12mo $2.50

Gilbart. A Practical Treatise on Banking.

By James William Gilbart, F R S. A new enlarged and improved edition Edited by J. Smith Homans, editor of "Banker's Magazine." To which is added "Money," by H. C. Carey. 8vo.............................$3.50

Gregory's Mathematics for Practical Men;

Adapted to the Pursuits of Surveyors, Architects, Mechanics, and Civil Engineers. 8vo., plates, cloth..........$2.50

Gas and Ventilation.

A Practical Treatise on Gas and Ventilation. By E. E Perkins. 12mo , cloth $1 25

Griswold. Railroad Engineer's Pocket Companion for the Field.

By W. Griswold. 12mo., tucks $1.25

Hartmann. The Practical Iron Manufacturer's Vade-mecum.

From the German of Dr. Carl Hartmann. Illustrated. (*In Press*)

Hay. The Interior Decorator:

The Laws of Harmonious Coloring adapted to Interior Decorations · with a Practical Treatise on House-Painting. By D. R Hay, House-Painter and Decorater. Illustrated by a Diagram of the Primary, Secondary, and Tertiary Colors. 12mo. (*In Press.*)

Inventor's Guide:

Patent Office and Patent Laws; or, a Guide to Inventors, and a Book of Reference for Judges, Lawyers, Magistrates, and others. By J. G. Moore. 12mo., cloth.. ....$1 25

Jervis. Railway Property.

A Treatise on the Construction and Management of Railways; designed to afford useful knowledge, in the popular style, to the holders of this class of property, as well as Railway Managers, Officers, and Agents By John B Jervis, late Chief Engineer of the Hudson River Railroad, Croton Aqueduct, etc. One volume, 12mo , cloth $2.00

CONTENTS.—Preface—Introduction. *Construction* —Introductory Land and Land Damages; Location of Line; Method of Business; Grading, Bridges and Culverts; Road Crossings, Ballasting Track , Cross Sleepers; Chairs and Spikes; Rails; Station Buildings; Locomotives, Coaches and Cars *Operating* —Introductory Freight; Passengers, Engine Drivers Repairs to Track, Repairs of Machinery; Civil Engineer, Superintendent; Supplies of Material, Receipts, Disbursements, Statistics, Running Trains, Competition, Financial Management, General Remarks.

Johnson. A Report to the Navy Department of the United States on American Coals,

Applicable to Steam Navigation, and to other purposes. By Walter R Johnson With numerous illustrations. 607 pp. 8vo., half morocco $6.00

Johnson. The Coal Trade of British America:

With Researches on the Characters and Practical Values of American and Foreign Coals. By Walter R. Johnson, Civil and Mining Engineer and Chemist. 8vo.............$2.00

Johnston. Instructions for the Analysis of Soils, Limestones, and Manures.

By J F. W Johnston 12mo.........................38

Kentish. A Treatise on a Box of Instruments,

And the Slide Rule; with the Theory of Trigonometry and Logarithms, including Practical Geometry, Surveying, Measuring of Timber, Cask and Malt Gauging, Heights and Distances. By Thomas Kentish. In one volume, 12mo..$1.25

Leroux. A Practical Treatise on Wools and Worsteds:

By Charles Leroux, Mechanical Engineer, and Superintendent of a Spinning Mill. Illustrated by 12 large plates and 34 engravings. *In Press*

CONTENTS.—Part I Practical Mechanics, with Formulæ and Calculations applicable to Spinning Part II Spinning of Combed, and Combed and Carded Wools on the Mule. Part III. French and English Spinning. Part IV Carded Wool.

Larkin. The Practical Brass and Iron Founder's Guide:

A Concise Treatise on Brass Founding, Moulding, the Metals and their Alloys, etc.: to which are added Recent Improvements in the Manufacture of Iron, Steel by the Bessemer Process, etc, etc By James Larkin, late Conductor of the Brass Foundry Department in Reaney, Neafie & Co.'s Penn Works Philadelphia. Fifth edition, revised, with Extensive Additions. In one volume, 12mo...................$2 25

Lieber. Assayer's Guide;

Or, Practical Directions to Assayers, Miners, and Smelters By Oscar M. Lieber. 12mo., cloth..................$1 25

Love. The Art of Dyeing, Cleaning, Scouring, and Finishing,

On the Most Approved English and French Methods: being Practical Instructions in Dyeing Silks, Woollens, and Cottons, Feathers, Chips Straw, etc.; Scouring and Cleaning Bed and Window Curtains, Carpets, Rugs, etc.; French and English Cleaning, any Color or Fabric of Silk, Satin, or Damask. By Thomas Love, a working Dyer and Scourer. In 1 vol., 12mo...................................$3.00

Lowig. Principles of Organic and Physiological Chemistry.

By Dr. Carl Lowig. Translated by Daniel Breed, M. D. 8vo., sheep..$3 50

Main and Brown. The Marine Steam-engine.

By Thomas J Main, Professor of Mathematics, Royal Naval College, and Thomas Brown, Chief Engineer, R. N. Illustrated by engravings and wood-cuts. 8vo, cloth $5.00

☞ THE TEXT BOOK OF THE UNITED STATES NAVAL ACADEMY.

CONTENTS—Introductory Chapter—The Boiler; The Engine, Getting up the Steam, Duties to Machinery when under Steam; Duties to Machinery during an Action or after an Accident, Duties to Engine, etc, on arriving in Harbor. Miscellaneous. Appendix.

Main and Brown. Questions on Subjects Connected with the Marine Steam-engine,

And Examination Papers, with hints for their Solution. By Thomas J. Main, Professor of Mathematics, Royal Naval College, and Thomas Brown, Chief Engineer R. N. 12mo., cloth..$1 50

Main and Brown. The Indicator and Dynamometer,

With their Practical Applications to the Steam-engine By Thomas J. Main and Thomas Brown. With Illustrations..$1.50

Makins. A Manual of Metallurgy,

More particularly of the Precious Metals, including the Methods of Assaying them. Illustrated by upwards of 50 engravings By George Hogarth Makins, M.R.C.S, F.C S., one of the Assayers to the Bank of England; Assayer to the Anglo-Mexican Mints, and Lecturer upon Metallurgy at the Dental Hospital, London. In one vol., 12mo...$3.50

CONTENTS.—General Properties of the Metals; General View of the Combining Properties of the Metals; Combination of Metals with the Non-Metallic Elements, Of Metallic Salts, Of Heating Apparatus, Furnaces, etc, Of Fuels Applicable to Metallurgic Operations; Metals of the First Class; Metals of the Second Class, The Principles of Electro-Metallurgy.

Marble Worker's Manual:

Containing Practical Information respecting Marbles in general, their Cutting, Working, and Polishing; Veneering, etc, etc. 12mo., cloth..$1.50

Molesworth. Pocket-book of Useful Formulæ and Memoranda for Civil and Mechanical Engineers.

By Guilford L. Molesworth, Member of the Institution of Civil Engineers, Chief Resident Engineer of the Ceylon Railway From the Tenth London edition $2.00

CONTENTS —*Civil Engineering*—Surveying, Levelling, Setting Out, etc ; Earthwork, Brickwork, Masonry, Arches, etc , Beams, Girders, Bridges, etc , Roofs, Floors, Columns, Walls, etc , Railways, Roads, Canals, Rivers, Docks, etc , Water-works, Sewers, Gas-works, Drainage, etc.; Warming Ventilation, Light, Sound, Heat, etc
Mechanical Engineering —Gravity, Mechanical Centres and Powers: Millwork, Teeth of Wheels, Shafting, Belting, etc , Alloys, Solders, and Workshop Recipes; Steam Boilers, and Steam-engines, Water-wheels, Turbines, etc , and Windmills, Paddle and Screw Steamers, Miscellaneous Machinery.
Weights and Measures, English and Foreign, Logarithms of Numbers; Triangles, Trigonometry, and Tables of Sines, etc ; Properties of Ellipse, Parabola, Circle, etc ; Mensuration of Surfaces and Solids; Tables of Areas, and Circumferences of Circles, Weights and Properties of Materials; Squares, Cubes, Powers, Roots, and Reciprocals of Numbers, Engineering Memoranda and Tables, Supplement by J T Hurst, C E , containing Additional Engineering Memoranda and Tables, Tables by Lewis Olrick, C E.

Miles. A Plain Treatise on Horse-shoeing.

With illustrations By William Miles, author of the "Horse's Foot" $1.00

Morfit. A Treatise on Chemistry,

Applied to the Manufacture of Soap and Candles · being a Thorough Exposition in all their Minutiæ of the Principles and Practice of the Trade, based upon the most recent Discoveries in Science and Art. By Campbell Morfit, Professor of Analytical and Applied Chemistry in the University of Maryland. A new and improved edition Illustrated with 260 engravings on wood. Complete in 1 volume, large 8vo... $20 00

Mortimer. The Pyrotechnist's Companion:

By G. W. Mortimer. Illustrated. 12mo , cloth...... $1 25

Napier. Manual of Electro-Metallurgy:

Including the Application of the Art to Manufacturing Processes. By James Napier From the second London edition, revised and enlarged Illustrated by engravings. In one volume, 12mo............................. $1 50

Napier. Chemistry Applied to Dyeing.

By James Napier, F. C. S Illustrated. 12mo $3.00

Nicholson. Bookbinding: A Manual of the Art of Bookbinding:

Containing full Instructions in the different Branches of Forwarding, Gilding, and Finishing. Also, the Art of Marbling Book-edges and Paper. By James B. Nicholson. Illustrated. 12mo., cloth $2.25

CONTENTS —Sketch of the Progress of Bookbinding, Sheet-work, Forwarding the Edges, Marbling, Gilding the Edges, Covering, Half Binding, Blank Binding, Boarding, Cloth-work, Ornamental Art, Finishing, Taste and Design, Styles, Gilding, Illuminated Binding, Blind Tooling, Antique, Coloring, Marbling, Uniform Colors, Gold Marbling, Landscapes, etc ; Inlaid Ornaments, Harmony of Colors, Pasting Down, etc , Stamp or Press-work, Restoring the Bindings of Old Books, Supplying imperfections in Old Books, Hints to Book-Collectors, Technical Lessons.

Norris. A Hand-book for Locomotive Engineers and Machinists.

By Septimus Norris, C. E. New edition, illustrated, 12mo., cloth $2 00

Nystrom. On Technological Education and the Construction of Ships and Screw Propellers for Naval and Marine Engineers.

By John W. Nystrom, late Acting Chief Engineer U. S. N. Second edition, revised with additional matter. Illustrated by 7 engravings 12mo. $2 50

CONTENTS —On Technological Education , The knowledge of Steam Engineering behind the knowledge of Science , Failure of Steamers for a want of Applied Science; Fresh water Condensers, and combustion of Fuel , Knowledge of Steamship Performance; Expansion experiments made by the Navy Department , Natural effect of Steam or maximum work per unit of Heat , Natural effect of Steam-engines , Nystrom's Pocket-book; Reform wanted in Scientific Books, America has taken the lead in Popular Education; Technological Institutions wanted , The National Academy of Sciences; Object of Technological Institutions , Steam-engineering and Ship-building; Necessity of complete Drawings before the building of Steamers is commenced , America has taken the lead in the new Naval Tactics; The Naval Academy, at Annapolis, not proper for a School of Steam-engineering; Want of applied Science in our Workshops , Locomotive Engineering, Communication to the Secretary of the Navy on the Science of Ship-building; Ship-builders consider their Art a Craft , Ship-builders' jealousy; Ship-building developed to the condition of a Science; Memorandum , Chief Engineer Isherwood does not approve the Parabolic Construction of Ships , On the Parabolic Construction of Ships; Application of the Parabolic Construction of Ships , Recording Formulas; Recording Tables; The labor of calculating the Ship-building Tables; Mr W L Hanscom, Naval Constructor, on the Parabolic Method; Mr J. Vaughan Merrick on the Parabolic Construction , Resignation, by the Author. as Acting Chief Engineer in the Navy; Memorandum; The Science of Dynamics in a confused condition , Illustrations required in Dynamics , Mr. Isherwood declines having the subject of Dynamics cleared up , The subject of Dynamics submitted to the National Academy of Sciences; On the elements of Dynamics; *force*, *power*, and *work*, defined; *Work*, a trinity of Physical Elements , Discussion with Naval Engineers on the subject of Dynamics , Questions in Dynamics submitted to the Academy of Sciences· Vis-viva; Unit for Power , Unit for Work, Navy Departmen attempting to reorganize the Corps of Engineers, Washington Navy Yard, Engineers in the Navy Department, Captain Fox on Engineering and the Construction of Ships, Secrecy respecting Ships' Drawings; Steam Boiler Explosions, Review of Screw Propellers, To Construct a Plain Screw, Propeller with a Compound Expanding Pitch, Propeller as Constructed by Chief Engineer Isherwood, Propeller as Constructed from Mr Isherwood's Drawings; Centripetal Propeller, Centripetal Propeller with Compound Expanding Pitch; The Office of the Coast Survey an example of what the Bureau of Steam-engineering should be, The Engineer-in-Chief of the Navy a Grand Admiral, Constructions ought not to be made in the Navy Department. The office of the Coast Survey and the Light-house Board naturally belong to the Navy.

O'Neill. Chemistry of Calico Printing, Dyeing, and Bleaching:

Including Silken, Woollen, and Mixed Goods; Practical and Theoretical. By Charles O'Neill. (*In Press*)

O'Neill. A Dictionary of Calico Printing and Dyeing.

By Charles O'Neill. (*In Press.*)

Painter, Gilder, and Varnisher's Companion.

Containing Rules and Regulations in every thing relating to the Arts of Painting, Gilding, Varnishing, and Glass Staining; numerous useful and valuable Receipts; Tests for the detection of Adulterations in Oils, Colors, etc.; and a statement of the Diseases and Accidents to which Painters, Gilders and Varnishers are peculiarly liable, with the simplest and best methods of Prevention and Remedy; with directions for Graining, Marbling, Sign Writing and Gilding on Glass. Tenth edition. To which are added complete Instructions for Coach Painting and Varnishing. 12mo, cloth.....$1.50

Pallett. The Miller's, Millwright's, and Engineer's Guide.

By Henry Pallett. Illustrated. In 1 vol, 12mo.......$3 00

CONTENTS.—Explanation of Characters used, Definitions of Words used in this Work, United States Weights and Measures, Decimal Fractions; On the Selection of Mill-stones, On the Dressing of New Mill-stones—making their Faces Straight, and ready for putting in the Furrows; Furrows: the manner of Laying them out their Draft, and cutting them in Directions for laying off and cutting the Holes for the Balance Ryne and Driver; Directions for putting in the Balance Ryne and the Boxes for the Driver, and making them fast, Of Setting the Bed Stone, and fastening the Bush therein, Directions how to Bridge or Tram the Spindle; Instructions for Grinding off the Lumps of New Stones, Turning the Back of the Running Stone, Rounding the Eye and Balancing the Stone, Directions for Dressing and Sharpening Mill-stones when they become dull, Respecting the Irons of the Mill, Description of Plate 4, Showing the Principle upon which the Mill-stones work, How to Fit a New Back on a Stone that has been Running; Of the Elevator, Conveyor, and Hopper Boy, Of Bolting Reels and Cloths, with Directions for Bolting and Inspecting Flour; Directions for Cleaning Wheat, Instructions for Grinding Wheat; Directions for Grinding Wheat with Garlic amongst it, and for Dressing the Stones suitable thereto, Directions how to put the Stones in Order for Grinding Wheat that has Garlic amongst it, Directions for Grinding Middlings, and how to Prevent the Stones from Choking, so as to make the most of them, Reels for Bolting the Middlings; Instructions for a small Mill, Grinding different kinds of Grain; Of the Manner of Packing Flour, Table Showing the number of Pounds which constitute a Bushel, as established by Law in the States therein named, The Duty of the Miller; Pearl Barley or Pot Barley, The Art of Distillation, Of the Importance of Draughting and Planning Mills Cogs: the best time for Seasoning and Cutting them, The Framing of Mill-work, Windmills, A Table of the Velocity of Wind; Instructions for Baking, Receipt for making Babbitt Metal, etc.; Cement, Solders, Table Showing the Product of a Bushel of Wheat of different Weights and Qualities, as ascertained from Experiments in Grinding Parcels, Of Saw-mills and their Management; The Circular Saw, Rules for Calculating the Speed the Stones and other pieces or parts of the Machinery run at, To find the Quantity, in Bushels, a Hopper will Contain, Table of Dry Measure; Spouts; the Necessity of making them Large, To lay off any required Angle Of Masonry; of Artificer's Work, Bricklayer's Work, Bricks and Lathes—Dimensions, Timber Measure; Table—Diameters in inches of Saw Logs reduced to inch board measure, Of the Wedge, Of Pumps, The Screw, Table showing the power of Man or Horse as applied to Machinery, Measure of Solidity, Rules for calculating Liquids, A Table showing the Capacity of Cisterns, Wells, etc., in Ale Gallons and Hogsheads, in proportion to their Diameters and Depths; Steel—Of the various degrees of Heat required in the Manufacture of Steel; Composition for Welding Cast Steel; Directions for Making and Sharpening Mill Picks, A Composition for Tempering Cast Steel Mill Picks; Governors for Flouring Mills, The Governor or Regulator, The Pulley, Of the Velocity of Wheels, Pulleys, Drums etc ; On Friction, Belting Friction: Of the Strength of different Bodies, Falling Bodies, Of the different Gearings for propelling Machinery, The Crown or Face Gearing On matching Wheels to make the Cogs wear even; On Steam and the Steam-engine, Of Engines—their Management, etc ; Prevention of Incrustation in Steam Boilers, Double Engines The Fly-wheel, Table of Circumferences and Areas of Circles, in Feet, suitable for Fly-wheels, etc , To calculate the effects of a Lever and Weight upon the Safety-valve of a Steam Boiler, etc.; Of the Slide Valve, Boilers, Chimneys; Explosion of Boilers· On the Construction of Mill-dams Rock Dam, Frame Dams, Brush or Log Dam; Gates, Description of Water-wheels; Of Non-elasticity and Fluidity in Impinging Bodies, Motion of Overshot Wheels; The Breast Wheel; Overshot or Breast Wheels, Table of the number of inches of water necessary to drive one run of Stones, with all the requisite Machinery for Grist and Saw-mills, under heads of water from four to thirty feet, Table containing the weight of columns of water, each one foot in length, and of various diameters; The Undershot Wheel, Tub Wheels, The Flutter Wheel, The Laws of Motion and Rest; Power of Gravity, Percussion, or Impulse, with the Reaction Attachment, Table of the velocities of the Combination Reaction Water-wheel per minute, from heads of from four to thirty feet, Tables to reckon the Price of Wheat from Thirty Cents to Two Dollars per Bushel

Pradal, Malepeyre and Dussauce. A Complete Treatise on Perfumery:

Containing Notices of the Raw Material used in the Art, and the best Formulæ According to the most approved methods followed in France, England, and the United States. By M P Pradal, Perfumer Chemist, and M. F. Malepeyre. Translated from the French, with extensive additions, by Professor H. Dussauce. 8vo. $7.50

CONTENTS.—Nature of the Trade of the Perfumer; Raw Material; Pomades; Almond Oils, Perfumed Oils, called Huile Antique, Powders Cosmetic Preparation for the Lips and Skin, Almond Pastes; Cosmetic Gloves Paints; Dentifrices; Volatile Oils; Aromatic Waters, Spirituous

Odors; Colors; Infusions; Tinctures; Spirits; Aromatic Alcohols; Fuming Pastils, Cloves; Sachets; Cosmetics, Cassolettes, Toilet Vinegars, Pharmaceutical Preparations made by the Perfumer, Toilet Soaps; Various Substances and Processes belonging to the Perfumer's Trade.

Proteaux. Practical Guide for the Manufacture of Paper and Boards.

By A. Proteaux, Civil Engineer, Graduate of the School of Arts and Manufactures, and Director of Thiers' Paper-mill, Puy-de-Dôme. With additions, by L. S Le Normand. Translated from the French with Notes, by Horatio Paine, A. B., M. D. To which is added a Chapter on the Manufacture of Paper from Wood in the United States, by Henry T. Brown, of the "American Artisan." Illustrated by six plates, containing Drawings of Raw Materials, Machinery, Plans of Paper-mills, etc., etc. 8vo..................$5 00

CONTENTS.—Chapt. I. *A Glance at the History of Paper-making.* Chapt II. *Raw Materials*—Rags Chapt. III. *Manufacture*—Sorting and Cutting; Dusting; Washing and Boiling; Reduction to Half-stuff; Drainage; Bleaching; Composition of the Pulp; Refining or Beating; Sizing; Coloring Matters; The Work of the Paper-machine, Finishing Chapt IV. *Manufacture of Paper from the Vat, or by Hand*—Manufacture of Paper by hand, Sizing; Finishing; Manufacture of Bank-note Paper, and Water-mark Paper in General; Comparison between Machine and Hand-made Papers, Classification of Paper Chapt V *Further Remarks on Sizing*—Of the Sizing-room, Method of Extracting Galatine; Operation of Sizing; Drying after Sizing: the Dutch method preferable to the French; Some important Observations upon Sizing; Appendix upon Sizing; Theories of Sizing, Sizing in the Pulp, M Canson's method of Sizing in the Pulp, Comparison of the Two methods Chapt VI *Different Substances Suitable for Making Paper*—Straw Paper, Wood Paper. Chapt VII *Chemical Analysis of Materials employed in Paper-making*—The Waters; Alkalimetrical Test; Examination of Limes; Chlorometric Tests; Examination of Manganese; Chlorometric Degrees of Samples of Manganese; Antichlorine, Alums; Kaolin; Starch; Coloring Materials, Fuel, Examination of Papers; Materials of a Laboratory. Chapt VIII *Working Stock of a Paper-mill*—Motive Power; Rag Cutters, Dusters; Washing Apparatus; Boiling Apparatus; Washing and Beating-engines; Apparatus for Bleaching and Draining the Pulp, Paper-machines; Finishing-machines, General Working Stock of a Paper-mill, General Remarks upon the Establishment of a Paper-mill, General Remarks in reference to Building; General Considerations. Chapt IX *The Manufacture of Paper from Wood in the United States* Chapt X. *Manufacture of Boards.* Chapt. XI *Manufacture of Paper in China and Japan.*

DESCRIPTION OF THE PLATES.

Regnault. Elements of Chemistry.

By M. V. Regnault. Translated from the French, by T. Forrest Betton, M. D, and edited, with notes, by James C. Booth, Melter and Refiner U. S. Mint, and Wm. L. Faber, Metallurgist and Mining Engineer. Illustrated by nearly 700 wood engravings. Comprising nearly 1,500 pages In two volumes, 8vo., cloth..........................$10 00

AMONG THE CONTENTS ARE—Volume I :French and English Weights, etc. Introduction—Crystallography, Chemical Nomenclature, Metalloids, Oxygen; Hydrogen; Selenium, Tellurium, Chlorine, Bromine; Iodine; Fluorine; Phosphorus; Arsenic, Boren; Silicum; Carbon, On the Equivalents of Metalloids. *Metals*—Geology; Physical Properties of the Metals; Chemical

Properties of the Metals. On Salts. I *Alkaline Metals*—Potassium; Sodium, Lithium, Ammonia. II *Alkalino-Earthy Metals*—Barium; Strontium; Calcium, Magnesium. III. *Earthy Metals*—Aluminum, Glucinum; Zirconium, Thorinum; Yttrium; Erbium; Terbium; Cerium, Lanthanum; Didymium. *Chemical Arts Dependent on the Preceding Bodies*—Gunpowder; Lime and Mortar; Glass; Kinds of Glass; Imperfections and Alterations of Glass; Pottery, the Paste of which becomes Compact by Burning, Pottery, the Paste of which remains Porous after Burning, Ornaments and Painting; Chemical Analysis of Earthenware.

Volume II.. Preparation of Ores, Manganese, Iron; Reduction in the Blast Furnace, Chromium; Cobalt; Nickel; Zinc, Cadmium; Tin; Titanium; Columbium; Niobium; Pelopium; Ilmenium, Lead, Metallurgy of; Bismuth, Metallurgy of; Antimony, Metallurgy of; Uranium; Tungsten; Molybdenum, Vanadium; Copper, Metallurgy of, Mercury, Metallurgy of; Silver, Metallurgy of; Gold, Metallurgy of; Platinum; Osmium; Iridium, Palladium; Rhodium, Ruthenium. IV. *Organic Chemistry*—Introduction—Ultimate Analysis of Organic Substances, Construction of a Formula; Analysis of Gases, Essential Proximate Principles of Plants, Acids Existing in Plants; Organic Alkaloids, Neutral Substances in Plants; Nitrils; Essential Oils; Products of Dry Distillation, Fats, Organic Coloring Mat-ers, Action of Plants on the Atmosphere, Animal Chemistry, Secretions, Excretions; Technical Organic Chemistry, Manufacture of Bread; Brewing; Cider and Perry, Wine-making; Beet Sugar, Cane Sugar; Sugar-refining, Manufacture of Bone Black, Soap-boiling; Principles of Dyeing; Mordants; Calico-printing; Tanning; Charring Wood and Coal, Manufacture of Illuminating Gas.

Sellers. The Color Mixer:

Containing nearly Four Hundred Receipts for Colors, Pastes, Acids, Pulps, Blue Vats, Liquors, etc., etc., for Cotton and Woollen Goods: including the celebrated Barrow Delaine Colors. By John Sellers, an experienced practical workman. In one volume, 12mo........................$2.50

Shunk. A Practical Treatise on Railway Curves and Location, for Young Engineers.

By Wm. F. Shunk, Civil Engineer. 12mo. $1.50

Smith. The Dyer's Instructor:

Comprising Practical Instructions in the Art of Dyeing Silk, Cotton, Wool and Worsted, and Woollen Goods: containing nearly 800 Receipts. To which is added a Treatise on the Art of Padding; and the Printing of Silk Warps, Skeins, and Handkerchiefs, and the various Mordants and Colors for the different styles of such work. By David Smith, Pattern Dyer. 12mo., cloth..............................$3 00

☞ This is by far the most valuable book of PRACTICAL RECEIPTS FOR DYERS ever published in this country—has been eminently popular, and the third edition is just now ready for delivery.

Strength and other Properties of Metals.

Reports of Experiments on the Strength and other Properties of Metals for Cannon. With a Description of the Machines for testing Metals, and of the Classification of

Cannon in service. By Officers of the Ordnance Department U. S Army. By authority of the Secretary of War. Illustrated by 25 large steel plates. In 1 vol., quarto.....$10.00

☞ The best treatise on cast-iron extant

Tables Showing the Weight of Round, Square, and Flat Bar Iron, Steel, etc.,

By Measurement. Cloth 63

Taylor. Statistics of Coal:

Including Mineral Bituminous Substances employed in Arts and Manufactures; with their Geographical, Geological, and Commercial Distribution and amount of Production and Consumption on the American Continent. With Incidental Statistics of the Iron Manufacture. By R. C. Taylor. Second edition, revised by S. S. Haldeman. Illustrated by five Maps and many Wood engravings. 8vo. cloth..............$6.00

Templeton. The Practical Examinator on Steam and the Steam-engine:

With Instructive References relative thereto, arranged for the use of Engineers, Students, and others. By Wm. Templeton, Engineer 12mo $1.25

This work was originally written for the author's private use. He was prevailed upon by various Engineers, who had seen the notes, to consent to its publication, from their eager expression of belief that it would be equally useful to them as it had been to himself

Turnbull. The Electro-Magnetic Telegraph:

With an Historical Account of its Rise, Progress, and Present Condition. Also, Practical Suggestions in regard to Insulation and Protection from the Effects of Lightning. Together with an Appendix, containing several important Telegraphic Devices and Laws. By Lawrence Turnbull, M. D, Lecturer on Technical Chemistry at the Franklin Institute Second edition Revised and improved Illustrated by numerous engravings. 8vo......................$2.50

Turner's (The) Companion:

Containing Instruction in Concentric, Elliptic, and Eccentric Turning; also, various Steel Plates of Chucks, Tools, and Instruments; and Directions for Using the Eccentric Cutter, Drill, Vertical Cutter and Rest; with Patterns and Instructions for working them. 12mo., cloth $1.50

Ulrich. Dussauce. A Complete Treatise on the Art of Dyeing Cotton and Wool,

As practiced in Paris, Rouen, Mulhausen, and Germany. From the French of M Louis Ulrich, a Practical Dyer in the principal Manufactories of Paris, Rouen, Mulhausen, etc., etc.; to which are added the most important Receipts for Dyeing Wool, as practiced in the Manufacture Impériale des Gobelins, Paris. By Prof. H. Dussauce 12mo...$3.00

Watson. Modern Practice of American Machinists and Engineers:

Including the Construction, Application and Use of Drills, Lathe Tools, Cutters for Boring Cylinders and Hollow Ware generally, with the most economical speed for the same; the results verified by Actual Practice at the Lathe, the Vice, and on the Floor. Together with Workshop Management, Economy of Manufactures, the Steam-engine, Boilers, Gears, Belting, etc, etc. By Egbert P. Watson, late editor of the "Scientific American." Illustrated with Eighty-six Engravings. In 1 volume, 12mo..........$2.50

CONTENTS.

PART 1.—The Drill and its Office.
PART 2.—Lathe Work.
PART 3.—Miscellaneous Tools and Processes.
PART 4.—Steam and Steam-engine.
PART 5.—Gears, Belting, and Miscellaneous Practical Information.

Watson. The Theory and Practice of the Art of Weaving by Hand and Power:

With Calculations and Tables for the use of those connected with the Trade By John Watson, Manufacturer and Practical Machine Maker. Illustrated by large drawings of the best Power-Looms. 8vo $5.00

Weatherly. Treatise on the Art of Boiling Sugar, Crystallizing, Lozenge-making, Comfits, Gum Goods,

And other processes for Confectionery, etc., in which are explained, in an easy and familiar manner, the various methods of manufacturing every description of raw and refined Sugar goods, as sold by Confectioners and others. 12mo. $2.00

Williams. On Heat and Steam:

Embracing New Views of Vaporization, Condensation, and Expansion. By Charles Wye Williams, author of a Treatise on the Cumbustion of Coal Chemically and Practically Considered. With Illustrations. 8vo. $3.50

Bullock. The American Cottage Builder:

A Series of Designs, Plans, and Specifications, from $200 to $20,000, for Homes for the People; together with Warming, Ventilation, Drainage, Painting, and Landscape Gardening. By John Bullock, Architect, Civil Engineer, Mechanician, and Editor of "The Rudiments of Architecture and Building," etc., etc. Illustrated by 75 engravings. In one vol., 8vo..$3 50

CONTENTS.—Chap. I.—*Generally*—Where to Build a Cottage; Bird Cottage; Objects Desired II —*The Various Parts*—Walls; Cob Walls, Mud Walls; Silverlocks' Hollow Walls; Dearnes' Hollow Brick Wall; Loudon's Hollow Brick Walls; Flint Built Walls; Walls of Framed Timber, Rubble, and Plaster; Walls of Hollow Bricks; Covering for External Walls; Inside Work; Floors; Lime-ash Floors, Concrete Floors; Plaster Floor; Asphalte; Floor of Hollow Pots, Tile Floor, Floors of Arched Brickwork in Mortar; Fire-proof Floor; Tile-trimmer; Girder Floor, Stairs formed of Tile; Roofs, Thatch, Tile for Roofing; Slate Roof, Cast-iron Roofing; Eaves-gutter; Chimney-shaft; Ventilation and Warming III —*Terra del Fuego Cottage.* IV —*Prairie Cottage*—Cottage of Unburnt Brick—Plan, Cross Section; Side View; Manner of Laying the Brick and the Foundation, Chimney-cap, Perspective, and Top Views. V —*The Farm Cottage*—Ground Floor, Attic Floor VI —*The Village Cottage.* VII —*Italian Cottage.* VIII. *Thatched Cottage* IX —*Cottage of the Society for Improving the Condition of the Poor.* X —*Warming and Ventilation*—Ventilation. XI.—*Model Cottage*—Hollow Brick Work XII —*Rural Cottage*—Basement Plan; Plan of the First Floor, Plan of the Second Floor. XIII.—*Octagon Cottage*—Plan of Basement; Plan of Principal Story. XIV.—*Drainage.* XV.—*Rural Homes*—Circumstances to be taken into consideration in the Choice of a Situation, Elevation; The character of the Surface on which to Build, Aspect, Soil and Subsoil; Water, Villa; Rural Home, No. 1, Views of a Suburban Residence in the English style; Rural Home, No. 2, Rural Home, No 3; Rural Home, No. 4 XVI —*Paint and Color.* XVII —*Suburban Residences*—Gothic Suburban Cottage of C Prescott, Esq, Troy, N Y; Basement, First Floor; Attic, Second Floor, Suburban Octagonal Cottage. XVIII.—*Landscape Gardening*—First steps in Forming a Landscape Garden; The Roads and Paths, Trees, Shrubs, and Planting, Hills and Mounds; Valleys and Low Grounds, Rock-work; Of Water, and its Appropriation or Adoption; Fountains; General Observations; Formal Gardening; Pleasure Grounds and Flower Gardens; The Flower Garden; The Greenhouse, The Conservatory XIX.—*Cost*—The Terra del Fuegan Cottage; The Prairie Cottage; The Village Cottage; The Italian Cottage, The Thatched Cottage, The Cottage of the Society for Improving the Condition of the Poor, Prince Albert's Model Cottage, The Rural Cottage; Mr Fowler's Octagonal Cottage; Rural Home, No 1; Rural Home, No 2; Rural Home, No 3; The Suburban Residence; The Octagonal Suburban Residence designed by Wilcox, The Byzantine Cottage, The Gothic Suburban Residence designed by Mr. Davis. XX —*Two Residences*—The Byzantine Cottage; Ground Plan; Plan of Second Story; The Gothic Suburban Residence of W H C. Waddell, Esq, N. Y., First Floor, Second Floor. XXI.—*Artist's and Artisan's Calling.*

Smeaton. Builder's Pocket Companion:

Containing the Elements of Building, Surveying, and Architecture; with Practical Rules and Instructions connected with the subject. By A. C. Smeaton, Civil Engineer, etc. In one volume, 12mo..............................$1 25

CONTENTS —The Builder, Carpenter, Joiner, Mason, Plasterer, Plumber, Painter, Smith, Practical Geometry, Surveyor, Cohesive Strength of Bodies, Architect.

A New Guide to the Sheet-iron and Boiler Plate Roller:

Containing a Series of Tables showing the weight of Slabs and Piles to Produce Boiler Plates, and of the weight of Piles and the sizes of Bars to produce Sheet-iron, the thickness of the Bar Gauge in decimals, the weight per foot, and the thickness on the Bar or Wire Gauge of the fractional parts of an inch, the weight per sheet, and the thickness on the Wire Gauge or Sheet-iron of various dimensions to weigh 112 lbs per bundle, and the conversion of Short Weight into Long Weight, and of Long Weight into Short. Estimated and collected by G. H. PERKINS and J. G. STOWE $2.50

CONTENTS.—Weight of Slabs to produce Boiler Plates (from 2 feet to 9½ feet, Superficial Measure, from ¼ inch to 1 inch in Thickness, allowing for Heating, Rolling, and Cropping). Weight of Slabs to produce Boiler Plates (from 10 feet to 18 feet, Superficial Measure, from ¼ inch to 1 inch in Thickness, allowing for Heating, Rolling, and Cropping). Weight of Piles to produce Boiler Plates (from 2 feet to 9½ feet, Superficial Measure, from ¼ inch to 1 inch in Thickness, allowing for Heating, Rolling, and Cropping). Weight of Piles to produce Boiler Plates (from 10 feet to 18 feet, Superficial Measure, from ¼ inch to 1 inch in Thickness, allowing for Heating, Rolling, and Cropping). Weight of Piles to produce Sheet Iron (from 2 feet to 9½ feet Superficial Measure, from 4 Wire Gauge to 14 Wire Gauge, allowing for Heating, Rolling, and Cropping). Weight of Piles to produce Sheet Iron (from 10 feet to 18 feet, Superficial Measure, from 4 Wire Gauge to 14 Wire Gauge, allowing for Heating, Rolling, and Cropping). Weight of Piles to produce Sheet Iron (from 2 feet to 9½ feet, Superficial measure, from 14 Wire Gauge to 30 Wire Gauge in thickness, allowing for Heating Rolling, and Cropping, both Bar and Sheet). Weight of Piles to produce Sheet Iron (from 10 feet to 18 feet, Superficial Measure, from 14 Wire Gauge to 30 Wire Gauge in Thickness, allowing for Heating, Rolling, and Cropping, both Bar and Sheet). Sizes of Bars to produce Sheet Iron (from 2 feet to 8 feet long, from 13 Wire Gauge to 20 Wire Gauge, allowing for Heating, Rolling, and Cropping). Sizes of Bars to produce Sheet Iron (from 2 feet to 8 feet long, from 21 Wire Gauge to 30 Wire Gauge, allowing for Heating, Rolling, and Cropping). Table showing the Thickness of the Bar Gauge in Decimals. Table showing the Weight per Foot, and the Thickness on the Bar or Wire Gauge of the Fractional Parts of an Inch. Table showing the Weight per Foot, and the Thickness on the Wire Gauge of the Fractional Parts of an Inch. Table showing the Weight per Sheet, and the Thickness on the Wire Gauge of Sheet Iron 2 feet long by 1½ feet wide, from 4 Sheets to 70 Sheets, to weigh 112 pounds per Bundle. Table showing the Weight per Sheet, and the Thickness on the Wire Gauge of Sheet Iron 2½ feet long by 2 feet wide, from 2 Sheets to 36 Sheets, to weigh 112 pounds per Bundle. Table showing the Weight per Sheet, and the Thickness on the Wire Gauge of Sheet Iron 4 feet long by 2 feet wide, from 1 Sheet to 28 Sheets, to weigh 112 pounds per Bundle. Table showing the Weight per Sheet, and the Thickness on the Wire Gauge of Sheet Iron 4 feet long by 2½ feet wide, from 1 Sheet to 23 Sheets, to weigh 112 pounds per Bundle. Table showing the Weight per Sheet, and the Thickness on the Wire Gauge of Sheet Iron 4 feet long by 3 feet wide, from 1 Sheet to 19 Sheets, to weigh 112 pounds per Bundle. Table showing the Weight per Sheet, and the Thickness on the Wire Gauge of Sheet Iron 5 feet long by 2 feet wide, from 1 Sheet to 23 Sheets, to weigh 112 pounds per Bundle. Table showing the Weight per Sheet, and the Thickness on the Wire Gauge of Sheet Iron 5 feet long by 2½ feet wide, from 1 Sheet to 18 Sheets, to weigh 112 pounds per bundle. Table showing the Weight per Sheet, and the Thickness on the Wire Gauge of Sheet Iron 5 feet long by 3 feet wide, from 1 Sheet to 15 Sheets, to weigh 112 pounds per Bundle. Table showing the Weight per Sheet, and the Thickness on the Wire Gauge of Sheet Iron 6 feet long by 2 feet wide, from 1 Sheet to 19 Sheets, to weigh 112 pounds per Bundle. Table showing the Weight per Sheet, and the Thickness on the Wire Gauge of Sheet Iron 6 feet long by 2½ feet wide, from 1 Sheet to 15 Sheets, to weigh 112 pounds per Bundle. Table showing the Weight per Sheet, and the Thickness on the Wire Gauge of Sheet Iron 6 feet long by 3 feet wide, from 1 Sheet to 12 Sheets, to weigh 112 pounds per bundle. Short Weight into Long. Long Weight into Short.

Rural Chemistry:

An Elementary Introduction to the Study of the Science in its Relation to Agriculture and the Arts of Life. By E Solly, Hon. Mem of Agr Society, England Large 12mo ...$1 50

CONTENTS.—*Introduction*—Chapt. I Objects of Chemistry Affinity, Nature of Combination and Decomposition, The Elements The Air, its Properties and Composition, Oxygen and Nitrogen Combustion, results of Combustion, Carbonic Acid Gas, Water, Ice, and Steam Effects of Frost, Latent Heat, Composition of Water, Hydrogen Chapt II—Carbon, its Different Forms, Cohesion, Combustion and Decay, Carbonic Acid Gas, produced by Respiration, Combustion Fermentation, etc. Nature of Acids and Salts, Carbonic Oxide, Carburetted Hydrogen, Fire Damp, Coal Gas, Compounds all definite, Combining Weights, Nitrogen combined with Hydrogen forms Ammonia: Carbonate. Sulphate, Muriate, and Phosphate of Ammonia; Nitric Acid; Nitrates; Sulphur, Sulphurous Acid, Sulphuric Acid, Sulphates, Sulphuretted Hydrogen, Chlorine, Muriatic Acid, Iodine, Bromine, Phosphorus, Phosphoric Acid Chapt III—Metals, Bases, Alkalies, Potash, its Properties, Carbonate and Nitrate of Potash, Gunpowder; Soda, Common Salt, Sulphate, Carbonate and Nitrate of Soda, The Alkaline Earths; Lime, its Nature and Properties, Carbonate, Sulphate, and Phosphate of Lime Magnesia, its Carbonate, Sulphate, Muriate, and Phosphate. Chapt IV.—The Earths, Alumina, its Properties, Alum, Silisia, or Silicic Acid; Silicates of Potash and Soda; Glass, Silicates in the Soil, in Plants, The Metals, their Oxides and Salts; Iron, its Oxides; Rusting of Iron; Pyrites, Sulphate of Iron, or Green Vitriol; Gold, Silver; Mercury, Copper; Sulphate of Copper, or Blue Vitriol; Zinc; Tin; Manganese; Lead, Metallic Alloys. Chapt V—Organic Matter, Vegetable Substances; Lignin, or Woody Fibre, Starch, Varieties of Starch; Gum, Soluble and insoluble; Sugar, Cane and Grape, its manufacture, Gluten, Albumen. Legumine, Fibrin, Gliadine, Chemical Transformations, Formation of Gum, Sugar, etc; Fermentation; Lactic Acid; Manufacture of Wine, Alcohol; Brandy and Grain Spirit; Brewing; Bread-making, Vinegar or Acetic Acid. Chapt VI.—Vegetable Principles; Vegetable Acids; Citric, Tartaric, Malic, and Oxalic Acids; Oils, fixed and volatile, Manufacture of Soap; Resins, Pitch and Tar, Coloring Matters, Dyeing; Inorganic Constituents of Plants, Animal Matter, Albumen; Fibrin; Caseine, Milk. Butter, and Cheese; Gelatine; Tanning, Leather; Fat; Bone, Protein, Food of Animals, Respiration, Circulation of the Blood, Digestion, Formation of Fat; Cookery, Roasting and Boiling; Action of Medicines Chapt VII—The Food of Plants; Substances Derived from the Air, Sources of Oxygen, Hydrogen, Nitrogen, and Carbon, Substances Derived from the Soil, Sources of Earthy Substances, Composition of Soils, their Formation Decomposition of Silicates, Mechanical Structure of Soils, The Saline Constituents of Soils, Organic Matters in Soils, Humus, Humic Acid, their use in Soils, Germination, Malting, Moisture, Air and Warmth, Influence of Light; Office of the Leaves, Roots, Formation of Organic Matter, Flowers, Fruit, Seeds, Organic and Organized Matter, Vitality of Embryo, Nature of Seeds, Earthy Substances in Plants, Effects of Climate, Action of Plants on the Air Chapt VIII.—Deterioration of Soils, its Cause, Modes of Maintaining the Fertility of the Soil, Theory of Fallowing, Rotation of Crops, Subsoil Ploughing, Draining, Manure, Organic Manure, Animal Manure, contains Nitrogen, Results of Putrefaction; Sulphuretted Hydrogen, Loss of Manure, Liquid Manure, Animal Excrements, Guano, Modes of Fixing Ammonia, by Acids, by Gypsum, etc, Strong Manures, Wool, Rags, Oil, Bones; Super-phosphate of Lime, Vegetable Manures; Sawdust, Seaweed, Green Manures, Irrigation; Inorganic Manures, Lime, Chalk, Marl, Shell Sand, Gypsum, Phosphate of Lime, Ashes, Burnt Clay, Soot, Charcoal, Gas Liquor, Potash, Alkaline Salts, Nitrates Common Salt, Salt and Lime Chapt IX—Composition of Particular Crops, Composition of Wheat, Barley, Oats, Rye; Maise, Rice, Buckwheat, Linseed, Hempseed, Oil-seeds; Beans; Peas; Lentils, Vetches, Potatoes, Batatas, Jerusalem Artichoke, Oxalis, Cabbage, Turnips, Mangel-Wurzel, Carrot, Parsnip, Clover, Lucern, Saintfoin; Composition of Particular Manures, Cows' Urine, Horse dung, Pigs' dung, Night-soil, Urine Bones of Oxen, Cows Horses, Pigs, Farmyard-dung, Guano, Wood-ashes, Lixiviated Ashes, Peat Ashes, Kelp. Index.

CPSIA information can be obtained at www.ICGtesting.com
Printed in the USA
BVOW06s0045220115

384437BV00013B/129/P